A CALL TO JOY

Timothy's Guide

Encouraging the Growing Believer

Billie Hanks, Jr.

 INTERNATIONAL EVANGELISM ASSOCIATION
SALADO, TEXAS 76571

 WORD MINISTRY RESOURCES
WACO, TX 76702

For more information about this ministry, write or call:

INTERNATIONAL EVANGELISM ASSOCIATION
PO BOX 1174
SALADO, TEXAS 76571
(254) 947-3030

Or visit us on the World Wide Web at WWW.IEAOM.ORG

Printed in the United States of America

This book is
dedicated
to those who love
the harvest.

CONTENTS

ACKNOWLEDGMENTS

For International Evangelism's staff, this new edition of *A Call To Joy* represents a milestone in our positive experience with follow-up. We would like to thank you for giving life to these materials by going through them, and seeking to grow in your Christian faith.

My personal thanks go to Rev. Sam Cook and our former staff members for their original contributions toward this effort. In addition, I would like to thank Mr. Randy Craig for his conceptual and editing skills, Rev. Dan Nelson for his creative and artistic gifts, and Mr. Randy Ray for his faithful support in typesetting and design. They have truly made this new edition a labor of love and dedication to Christ.

The literary skills and disciple-making experience of Robert Coleman, LeRoy Eims, Gary Kuhne, and Gene Warr offer invaluable insight and inspiration to this basic New Testament emphasis on follow-up and discipleship.

My prayer is that each person who uses *A Call To Joy* will experience the great satisfaction that comes from knowing, learning, and serving the Lord Jesus Christ.

Yours in that joy,

Billie Hanks, Jr.

SESSION ONE DISCUSSION GUIDE

WELCOME TO *A CALL TO JOY*

In celebration of your desire to grow in the Christian life, you will not only receive this book, but much more importantly, receive a friend! Each time you meet together you can enjoy Christian fellowship. During your times of discussion, prayer, and Bible study, you will have the opportunity of knowing one another better.

Normally, it takes from seven to ten weeks to cover this inspirational material. We pray that these will be some of the most rewarding and enjoyable weeks you have ever experienced. James 4:8 says, *"Draw near to God and He will draw near to you."*

This first meeting will be very different from the rest because we want to be sure that a new church member has a clear understanding of what it means to know Christ as their personal Savior. We trust that you will be enriched by this basic study, even if you have already understood all or part of it's essential message.

1

UNDERSTANDING THE GOSPEL

A. Mankind's Spiritual Need.

"As it is written, 'There is none righteous, not even one.'" (Romans 3:10)

The account of man's initial disobedience to God is recorded in Genesis 2 and 3.

1. *"And the Lord God commanded the man, 'You are free to eat from any tree in the garden; but you must not eat from the tree of the knowledge of good and evil, for when you eat of it you will surely die.'"* (Genesis 2:16 & 17, NIV)

2. *"Therefore, just as through one man sin entered the world, and death through sin, and thus death spread to all men, because all sinned."* (Romans 5:12, NKJV)

3. *"For all have sinned and fall short of the glory of God."* (Romans 3:23)

B. Consequences of Disobedience.

Man chose to disobey God, and consequence always follows choice!

There are two kinds of death explained in the Bible. One is *physical*, which we will look at in a moment, and the other is *spiritual*, which the Bible is talking about in Romans 6:23.

1. *"For the wages of sin is death, but the gift of God is eternal life in Christ Jesus our Lord."* (Romans 6:23, NKJV)

2. *"And as it is appointed for men to die once, but after this the judgement."* (Hebrews 9:27, NKJV)

C. God's Provision.

Man's sin called for judgment. Yet God's love for man called for forgiveness. God remained true to His character of being just and loving by paying sin's penalty Himself.

1. *"But God demonstrates His own love toward us, in that while we were still sinners, Christ died for us."* (Romans 5:8, NKJV)

2. *"For Christ died for sins once for all, the righteous for the unrighteous, to bring you to God. He was put to death in the body but made alive by the Spirit."* (1 Peter 3:18, NIV)

3. *"For by grace you have been saved through faith, and that not of yourselves; it is the gift of God, not of works, lest anyone should boast."* (Ephesians 2:8 & 9, NKJV)

D. Man's Response.

Christ has come and revealed God. His death has satisfied God's righteousness and justice. Through Christ we can have our sins forgiven, be in right standing with God, and have eternal life. But we are not forced to believe or to accept God's mercy and grace. The choice is ours.

1. *"Now after John was put in prison, Jesus came to Galilee, preaching the gospel of the Kingdom of God, and saying, 'The time is fulfilled, and the kingdom of God is at hand. Repent, and believe in the gospel.'"* (Mark 1:14 & 15, NKJV)

2. *"Yet to all who received Him, to those who believed in His name, He gave the right to become children of God."* (John 1:12, NIV)

3. You must _____ *and* _____.

First you must *believe* that Jesus is *who* He claimed to be. He was born of a virgin, lived a sinless life, paid the penalty for our sins, and rose from the dead. He said He came to *seek* and *save* the lost, and to be our Savior.

Next, you must *receive* Him as your own personal Savior.

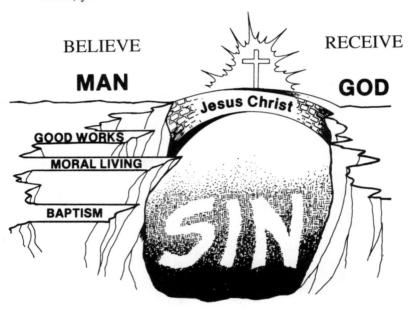

A PRAYER FOR SALVATION

"Lord Jesus, I am a sinner, . . .	**Confession**
but I am sorry for my sins.	**Contrition**
I want to turn from my sins; I am willing	**Repentance**
to begin a new life with Your help.	
Lord Jesus, please come into my heart and	**Invitation**
life right now.	
From this moment forward, my life belongs	**Consecration**
to You and You alone.	
I will love You, serve You, tell others	**Dependence**
about You, and trust You to live	
Your life through me.	
Thank You Lord, for coming into my	**Thanksgiving**
life and for forgiving my sins today."	

4. *"He who has the Son has life; he who does not have the Son of God does not have life. These things I have written to you who believe in the name of the Son of God, that you may know that you have eternal life, and that you may continue to believe in the name of the Son of God."* (1 John 5:12 & 13, NKJV)

5. *"For God so loved the world that He gave His only begotten Son, that whoever believes in Him should not perish but have everlasting life."* (John 3:16, NKJV)

6. *"In Him we have redemption through His blood, the forgiveness of sins, according to the riches of His grace."* (Ephesians 1:7, NKJV)

Although man was created without knowledge of evil, he yielded to Satan's temptation and chose to know both good and evil. The consequence of this choice was spiritual death – separation from God. God's response was to judge mankind for disobedience and provide salvation through Christ. By receiving Christ, a person receives forgiveness of sin and becomes a child of God for eternity!

USING THE NOTE-TAKING SECTION OF YOUR *SPIRITUAL JOURNAL*

Psychologists tell us that after 72 hours, we normally remember:

Only about _____ of what we hear.
Only about _____ of what we read.
About _____ of what we hear and read.
About _____ of what we hear, read, and do!

This study was conducted by the United States Air Force.

THE IMPORTANCE OF BECOMING INVOLVED IN A LOCAL CHURCH

1. *"And they were continually devoting themselves to the apostles' teaching and to fellowship, to the breaking of bread and to prayer."* (Acts 2:42)

2. *"Let us not give up meeting together, as some are in the habit of doing, but let us encourage one another – and all the more as you see the Day approaching."* (Hebrews 10:25, NIV)

3. *"And He gave some as apostles, and some as prophets, and some as evangelists, and some as pastors and teachers, for the equipping of the saints for the work of service, to the building up of the body of Christ."* (Ephesians 4:11 & 12)

TIMOTHY'S WEEKLY SPIRITUAL GROWTH ASSIGNMENT:

Timothy: You will notice that your book contains several blanks. These blanks are to be filled in *during each session* with your Discipler, not as a homework assignment.

A. Read a Quiet Time each morning this week, starting on page 78. Mark highlights as you read and be prepared to share them next week. You may wish to mark highlights by putting an "*" at the start of a highlight, and a ")" at the end. Pray the suggested prayer to God at the end of your Quiet Time. You may wish to pray this prayer aloud.

B. Read Chapter 1, "The Love of God," starting on page 39. Mark highlights as you read and be prepared to share them next week.

C. Take sermon notes using your *Spiritual Journal* and be prepared to share highlights next week. If you have questions about the sermon, be sure to write them down. You can ask your Discipler about them during your next session.

D. Start reading the Gospel of John *at your own pace*. If you have any questions as you read, write them in the note-taking section of your *Spiritual Journal*. Ask your Discipler to answer them during your next session.

DISCUSS LAST WEEK'S ASSIGNMENTS

WHAT DOES THE BIBLE SAY ABOUT SALVATION?

A. **1 John 5:11-13:** *"And the witness is this, that God has given us eternal life, and this life is in His Son. He who has the Son has the life; he who does not have the Son of God does not have the life. These things I have written to you who believe in the name of the Son of God, in order that you may know that you have eternal life."*

God wants you to *know for certain* that you are a Christian!

B. **There is a difference between** _____ **and** _____ .

ILLUSTRATION: _____

_____

When I am out of fellowship with God, I may have false
_____.

We need to _____ and accept
_____ promise, rather than our feelings as the basis for our
assurance of salvation.

ILLUSTRATION: _____

We can _____ in God's forgiveness and _____
in His salvation!

HOW DO I SHARE MY DECISION WITH FAMILY AND FRIENDS?

Be _____ and _____.

Billy Graham has said, "The true test of every Christian is the way
he_____."

WHAT IS A DAILY QUIET TIME?

DEFINITION: A Quiet Time is a part of your day which is set
aside for _____. It normally
includes Bible reading, prayer, and a decision to apply a Scriptural
insight.

Psalm 46:10a says, *"Be still, and know that I am God . . ."* (KJV)

ILLUSTRATION: _____

Our daily danger is becoming _____ for God to *bless* us!

WHY HAVE A DAILY QUIET TIME?

A. To help fulfill your highest purpose.

"God is faithful, through whom you were called into fellowship with His Son, Jesus Christ our Lord." (1 Corinthians 1:9)

Every Christian has a high calling: _____with Christ!

B. To follow the Lord's example.

"Very early in the morning, while it was still dark, Jesus got up, left the house and went off to a solitary place, where He prayed." (Mark 1:35, NIV)

"Yet the news about Him spread all the more, so that crowds of people came to hear Him and to be healed of their sicknesses. But Jesus often withdrew to lonely places and prayed." (Luke 5:15 & 16, NIV)

For the Lord Jesus, having Quiet Times was an absolute _____.

C. To gain spiritual strength.

"I have not departed from the commandment of His lips; I have treasured the words of His mouth more than my necessary food." (Job 23:12, NKJV)

Jesus said, *"Man does not live by bread alone, but on every word that comes from the mouth of God."* (Matthew 4:4b, NIV)

The Bible is our source of spiritual _____ and _____.

TIMOTHY'S WEEKLY SPIRITUAL GROWTH ASSIGNMENT:

A. Continue reading your Quiet Times each morning. Start writing a Scriptural insight and prayer for each day. Be prepared to share them next week.

B. Read Chapter 2, "Learning to Walk," starting on page 45. Mark highlights as you read and be prepared to share them next week.

C. Take sermon notes using your *Spiritual Journal* and be prepared to share highlights next week.

D. Read *Steps to Peace with God* and stop to thank Him for your personal salvation!

E. Continue reading the Gospel of John at your own pace.

SESSION THREE DISCUSSION GUIDE

3

DISCUSS LAST WEEK'S ASSIGNMENTS

WHAT ARE THE PRACTICAL BENEFITS OF NOTE-TAKING?

"So then faith comes by hearing, and hearing by the word of God." (Romans 10:17, NKJV)

A. My faith _____ each time I hear God's Word.

B. We take notes because of a basic human problem — _____ .

    ILLUSTRATION:_____.

Note-taking helps you:

1. _____ more intently.

2. _____ what you hear.

3. _____ the message to your life.

4. _____ the truth with others.

YOU CAN DEVELOP AN EFFECTIVE DAILY QUIET TIME

A. By discovering its practical benefits for yourself.

1. It is a key to fulfilling _____ for your life.

    *"Do not let this Book of the Law depart from your mouth;
    meditate on it day and night, so that you may be careful to
    do everything written in it. Then you will be prosperous and
    successful."* (Joshua 1:8, NIV)

2. It is the means used by The Holy Spirit to reveal the
    _____ , _____ or _____
    in your life which He wants to help you develop or change.

    King David prayed, *"Search me, O God, and know my heart;
    test me and know my anxious thoughts. See if there is any
    offensive way in me, and lead me in the way everlasting."*
    (Psalm 139: 23 & 24 , NIV)

3. It prepares you to be used in the lives of _____.

    *"When they saw the courage of Peter and John and realized
    that they were unschooled, ordinary men, they were aston-
    ished and they took note that these men had been with
    Jesus."* (Acts 4:13, NIV)

4. It provides the opportunity for _____ with
    our Lord.

Jesus said, ". . . *I am with you always, to the very end of the age.*" (Matthew 28:20, NIV)

B. By anticipating your Quiet Times in faith!

1. _____ God to meet with you and guide you through _____.

   "*I will instruct you and teach you in the way you should go.*" (Psalm 32:8a, NIV)

   "*Thy word is a lamp to my feet, and a light to my path.*" (Psalm 119:105)

   "*He awakens me morning by morning, He awakens my ear to listen as a disciple.*" (Isaiah 50:4b)

2. Determine to be _____ .

   ILLUSTRATION: _____ .

   The apostle Paul said, ". . . *discipline yourself for the purpose of godliness.*" (1 Timothy 4:7b)

   "*Let us not grow weary while doing good, for in due season we shall reap if we do not lose heart.*" (Galatians 6:9, NKJV)

   ILLUSTRATION: _____ .

3. Always _____ the insights God gives you in your Quiet Time.

   "*Do not merely listen to the word, and so deceive yourselves. Do what it says.*" (James 1:22, NIV)

   You can expect His correction to include:

   a. _____ you either need to *start or stop.*

   b. _____ you need to either *develop or change.*

C. By planning ahead for success.

1. Get a good night's _____, so you wake up refreshed.

   "How long will you lie there, you sluggard? When will you get up from your sleep?" (Proverbs 6:9, NIV)

2. _____ your day with Christ!

   David, the Psalmist, said, *"In the morning, O Lord, you hear my voice."* (Psalm 5:3a, NIV)

3. Select a special _____ .

HOW DO YOU SUSTAIN YOUR PERSONAL DISCIPLINE AND GROWTH?

"He who walks with wise men will be wise. . ." (Proverbs 13:20a)

ILLUSTRATION: _____

Remember that growth comes _____ , so be patient and enjoy each new day of fellowship with God and other Christians.

TIMOTHY'S WEEKLY SPIRITUAL GROWTH ASSIGNMENT:

A. Continue your daily Quiet Times each morning. Write a Scriptural insight, prayer, and application for each day. Be prepared to share them next week.

B. Read Chapter 3, "The Perfect Example," starting on page 53. Mark highlights for discussion next week.

C. Take sermon notes using your *Spiritual Journal,* and come prepared to share your favorite highlights.

D. Continue reading the Gospel of John at your own pace.

SESSION FOUR DISCUSSION GUIDE

DISCUSS LAST WEEK'S ASSIGNMENTS

THE PRIVILEGE OF SHARING GOD'S GOOD NEWS

"Therefore go and make disciples of all nations, baptizing them in the name of the Father and of the Son and of the Holy Spirit, and teaching them to obey everything I have commanded you. And surely I am with you always, to the very end of the age." (Matthew 28:19 & 20, NIV)

"But you will receive power when the Holy Spirit comes on you; and you will be My witnesses in Jerusalem, and in all Judea and Samaria, and to the ends of the earth." (Acts 1:8, NIV)

Using an evangelistic booklet:

A. **Keeps you focused on the** _____.

B. **Insures the availability of** _____.

C. **Allows the inquirer to**_____**the message.**

D. **Provides**_____ **assistance to underscore the verbal message.**

THE PRIVILEGE OF PRAYER

A. **The nature of prayer.**

Prayer has been defined as "Man's conversation with God."

ILLUSTRATION: _____

1. Through prayer, we can talk with God about

    _____ , _____ ,

    _____ .

2. Prayer involves both _____ and _____ to God.

B. **The Lord Jesus' prayer life.**

1. He prayed in the _____ .

    "Very early in the morning, while it was still dark, Jesus got up, left the house and went off to a solitary place, where He prayed." (Mark 1:35, NIV)

2. He prayed _____.

    "Yet the news about Him spread all the more, so that crowds of people came to hear Him and to be healed of their sicknesses. But Jesus often withdrew to lonely places and prayed." (Luke 5:15 & 16, NIV)

3. He earnestly prayed _____ making major decisions.

"One of those days Jesus went out to a mountainside to pray, and spent the night praying to God. When morning came, He called His disciples to Him and chose twelve of them, whom He also designated apostles." (Luke 6:12 & 13, NIV)

C. Make prayer a consistent priority of your life.

1. Prayer is an alternative to _____.

"Do not be anxious about anything, but in everything, by prayer and petition, with thanksgiving, present your requests to God." (Philippians 4:6, NIV)

2. Prayer is a means of avoiding _____.

"Watch and pray so that you will not fall into temptation. The spirit is willing, but the body is weak." (Matthew 26:41, NIV)

3. Prayer is a means of great_____.

"The prayer of a righteous man is powerful and effective." (James 5:16b, NIV)

TIMOTHY'S WEEKLY SPIRITUAL GROWTH ASSIGNMENT:

A. Continue your daily Quiet Times using your *Timothy's Guide* and *Spiritual Journal.* Be prepared to share your insights next week.

B. Prayerfully give a copy of *Steps to Peace with God* to someone this week. If they seem open to talk, simply pray silently for guidance and let the conversation develop naturally.

C. Read Chapter 4, "The Secret of Godliness," starting on page 59. Mark highlights and be prepared to share them next week.

D. Take sermon notes using your *Spiritual Journal.* Be prepared to discuss your highlights next week.

E. Continue reading the Gospel of John at your own pace.

DISCUSS LAST WEEK'S ASSIGNMENT

DEVELOPING A LIFE OF PEACE THROUGH PRAYER

A. Maintain a proper attitude.

   1. Be honest and transparent when you pray.

      "All my longings lie open before You, O Lord; my sighing is not hidden from You." (Psalm 38:9, NIV)

      David knew that _____ in his life was hidden from God.

   2. Keep your prayers simple.

"'Abba, Father, all things are possible unto Thee; take away this cup from Me: nevertheless not what I will, but what Thou wilt.'" (Mark 14:36, KJV)

God wants us to talk to Him with the same sincerity that a child expresses toward his loving _____.

3. Pray with pure motives.

"When you ask, you do not receive, because you ask with wrong motives . . ." (James 4:3a, NIV)

"All a man's ways seem innocent to him, but motives are weighed by the Lord." (Proverbs 16:2, NIV)

Our prayers are no better than _____ for praying.

B. Make prayer a natural part of your life.

1. Pray _____ the day.

"Pray continually." (1 Thessalonians 5:17, NIV)

2. It has been wisely said that a Christian will either pray for _____ throughout the day or_____ at night!

3. We need to _____ before _____, and pray about both _____ and _____ needs.

"Do not be anxious about anything, but in everything, by prayer and petition, with thanksgiving, present your requests to God. And the peace of God, which transcends all understanding, will guard your hearts and your minds in Christ Jesus." (Philippians 4:6 & 7, NIV)

ILLUSTRATION: _____

4. Pray _____, in faith.

> *"And she made a vow, saying, 'O Lord Almighty, if You will only look upon Your servant's misery and remember me, and not forget Your servant but give her a son, then I will give him to the Lord for all the days of his life, and no razor will ever be used on his head.'"* (1 Samuel 1:11, NIV)

Vague universal prayers make it _____ to _____ and appreciate God's answers.

C. Learn the Biblical guidelines for prayer.

> *"If My people, who are called by My name, will humble themselves and pray and seek My face and turn from their wicked ways, then will I hear from heaven and will forgive their sin and will heal their land."* (2 Chronicles 7:14, NIV)

> *"If I had cherished sin in my heart, the Lord would not have listened."* (Psalm 66:18, NIV)

We must desire and seek a clean _____ in preparation for a life of effective prayer.

D. Appreciate the different dimensions of prayer.

1. _____ - Praising God for who He is.

2. _____ - Agreeing with God about your sin.

3. _____ - Thanking God for what He has done.

4. _____ - Praying for the needs of others.

5. _____ - Praying for your personal needs.

TIMOTHY'S WEEKLY SPIRITUAL GROWTH ASSIGNMENT:

A. Continue your daily Quiet Times using your *Spiritual Journal*, Bible, and Quiet Time Reading Guide on page 109. Be prepared to share your insights next week.

B. Give another copy of *Steps to Peace with God* to someone this week.

C. Read Chapter 5, "Principles for Living in Victory," starting on page 67. Mark highlights and be prepared to share them next week.

D. Take sermon notes using your *Spiritual Journal*. Be prepared to share your highlights next week.

E. List the name of one individual or ministry for each day of the week using the Intercession Section of your *Spiritual Journal* on pages 14-17.

F. Continue reading the Gospel of John at your own pace.

SESSION SIX DISCUSSION GUIDE

6

DISCUSS LAST WEEK'S ASSIGNMENTS

THE MINISTRY OF THE HOLY SPIRIT

"I have been crucified with Christ; and it is no longer I who live, but Christ lives in me; and the life which I now live in the flesh I live by faith in the Son of God, who loved me, and delivered Himself up for me." (Galatians 2:20)

God is a Trinity consisting of God the Father, God the Son, and God the Holy Spirit. It is through the ministry of the Holy Spirit that Christ indwells believers and empowers us for Christian service.

"For it is God who works in you to will and to act according to His good purpose." (Philippians 2:13, NIV)

ILLUSTRATION: _____.

"If anyone does not have the Spirit of Christ, he does not belong to Christ." (Romans 8:9b, NIV)

A. The Holy Spirit _____ all genuine believers.

"Because you are sons, God sent the Spirit of His Son into our hearts, the Spirit who calls out, 'Abba, Father.'" (Galatians 4:6, NIV)

"Guard the good deposit that was entrusted to you – guard it with the help of the Holy Spirit who lives in us." (2 Timothy 1:14, NIV)

B. The Holy Spirit is active in the entire salvation process.

1. He _____ the world of sin.

    "And He, when He comes, will convict the world concerning sin, and righteousness, and judgment." (John 16:8)

2. He _____ Christ.

    "When the Counselor comes, whom I will send to you from the Father, the Spirit of truth who goes out from the Father, He will testify about Me." (John 15:26, NIV)

    "He shall glorify Me; for He shall take of Mine, and shall disclose it to you." (John 16:14)

3. He uses the _____ as a sword.

"And take the helmet of salvation, and the sword of the Spirit, which is the word of God." (Ephesians 6:17)

4. He _____ people to the truth.

"And the Spirit and the bride say, 'Come.' And let the one who hears say, 'Come.' And let the one who is thirsty come; let the one who wishes take the water of life without cost." (Revelation 22:17)

"You men who are stiff-necked and uncircumcised in heart and ears are always resisting the Holy Spirit; you are doing just as your fathers did." (Acts 7:51)

5. He _____us from the bondage of legalism so we can enjoy the grace of God.

"Now the Lord is the Spirit; and where the Spirit of the Lord is, there is liberty." (2 Corinthians 3:17)

"But if you are led by the Spirit, you are not under the Law." (Galatians 5:18)

6. He _____ us, and enables us to become born-again followers of Christ.

"But when the kindness and love of God our Savior appeared, He saved us, not because of righteous things we had done, but because of His mercy. He saved us through the washing of rebirth and renewal by the Holy Spirit, whom He poured out on us generously through Jesus Christ our Savior." (Titus 3:4-6, NIV)

7. He comes to _____ at the moment of our salvation.

"Peter replied, 'Repent and be baptized, every one of you, in the name of Jesus Christ for the forgiveness of your sins. And you will receive the gift of the Holy Spirit.'" (Acts 2:38, NIV)

8. He _____ our future with Christ in heaven!

*"In Him, you also, after listening to the message of truth, the
gospel of your salvation – having also believed, you were
sealed in Him with the Holy Spirit of promise, who is given
as a pledge of our inheritance, with a view to the redemption
of God's own possession, to the praise of His glory."*
(Ephesians 1:13 & 14)

9. He gives us _____ of salvation.

*"The Spirit Himself bears witness with our spirit that we
are children of God."* (Romans 8:16)

*"By this we know that we abide in Him and He in us, because
He has given us of His Spirit."* (1 John 4:13)

C. The Holy Spirit empowers us to _____with boldness!

*"But you shall receive power when the Holy Spirit has come
upon you; and you shall be My witnesses both in Jerusalem, and
in all Judea and Samaria, and even to the remotest part of the
earth."* (Acts 1:8)

D. The Holy Spirit is our _____ .

*"But I tell you the truth, it is to your advantage that I go away;
for if I do not go away, the Helper shall not come to you; but if
I go, I will send Him to you."* (John 16:7)

ILLUSTRATION: _____ .

E. The Holy Spirit empowers us to develop a godly character.

1. He transforms us into the _____ .

"And we . . . are being transformed into His likeness with ever-increasing glory, which comes from the Lord, who is the Spirit." (2 Corinthians 3:18, NIV)

2. He empowers us to exemplify godly _____ qualities and _____ .

"But the fruit of the Spirit is love, joy, peace, patience, kindness, goodness, faithfulness, gentleness, self-control; against such things there is no law." (Galatians 5:22 & 23)

3. He gives us _____ .

"I pray that out of His glorious riches He may strengthen you with power through His Spirit . . ." (Ephesians 3:16, NIV)

4. He enables us to overflow with _____ !

"May the God of hope fill you with all joy and peace as you trust in Him, so that you may overflow with hope by the power of the Holy Spirit." (Romans 15:13, NIV)

5. He fills us with _____ !

"And the disciples were continually filled with joy and with the Holy Spirit." (Acts 13:52)

F. The Holy Spirit helps us _____ .

"But I say, walk by the Spirit, and you will not carry out the desire of the flesh." (Galatians 5:16)

"Those who live according to the sinful nature have their minds set on what that nature desires; but those who live in accordance with the Spirit have their minds set on what the Spirit desires. The mind of sinful man is death, but the mind controlled by the Spirit is life and peace." (Romans 8:5 & 6, NIV)

G. The Holy Spirit _____ us.

"But the Counselor, the Holy Spirit, whom the Father will send in My name, will teach you all things." (John 14:26a, NIV)

"We have not received the spirit of the world but the Spirit who is from God, that we may understand what God has freely given us." (1 Corinthians 2:12, NIV)

H. The Holy Spirit _____ us where and how to share our Christian witness.

"The Spirit told Philip, 'Go to that chariot and stay near it.' Then Philip ran up to the chariot and heard the man reading Isaiah the prophet. 'Do you understand what you are reading?' Philip asked. 'How can I,' he said, 'unless someone explains it to me?' So he invited Philip to come up and sit with him." (Acts 8:29-31, NIV)

"Paul and his companions traveled throughout the region of Phrygia and Galatia, having been kept by the Holy Spirit from preaching the word in the province of Asia. When they came to the border of Mysia, they tried to enter Bithynia, but the Spirit of Jesus would not allow them to." (Acts 16:6 & 7, NIV)

"The Spirit told me to have no hesitation about going with them. These six brothers also went with me, and we entered the man's house." (Acts 11:12, NIV)

I. The Holy Spirit helps us receive _____ into our hearts.

"And hope does not disappoint us, because God has poured out His love into our hearts by the Holy Spirit, whom He has given us." (Romans 5:5, NIV)

J. The Holy Spirit _____ us.

"Who have been chosen according to the foreknowledge of God the Father, through the sanctifying work of the Spirit, for obedience to Jesus Christ and sprinkling by His blood." (1 Peter 1:2, NIV)

K. The Holy Spirit _____ us and baptizes us into one body.

"For by one Spirit we were all baptized into one body, whether Jews or Greeks, whether slaves or free, and we were all made to drink of one Spirit." (1 Corinthians 12:13)

L. The Holy Spirit compassionately _____ for us as we pray.

"In the same way, the Spirit helps us in our weakness. We do not know what we ought to pray for, but the Spirit Himself intercedes for us with groans that words cannot express. And He who searches our hearts knows the mind of the Spirit, because the Spirit intercedes for the saints in accordance with God's will." (Romans 8:26 & 27, NIV)

M. The Holy Spirit empowers us to _____ false teachers.

"Then Saul, who was also called Paul, filled with the Holy Spirit, looked straight at Elymas and said, 'You are a child of the devil and an enemy of everything that is right! You are full of all kinds of deceit and trickery. Will you never stop perverting the right ways of the Lord?'" (Acts 13:9 & 10, NIV)

N. The Holy Spirit is actively involved in the _____ of all believers.

"And if the Spirit of Him who raised Jesus from the dead is living in you, He who raised Christ from the dead will also give life to your mortal bodies through His Spirit, who lives in you." (Romans 8:11, NIV)

O. The Holy Spirit empowers Christians to carry out certain ministries for the common good.

These ministries are called _____ .
They are listed in Romans Chapter 12, 1 Corinthians Chapter 12, and Ephesians Chapter 4. Every Christian has at least one of these gifts.

"Now to each one the manifestation of the Spirit is given for the common good." (1 Corinthians 12:7, NIV)

P. The Holy Spirit _____ .

"And do not get drunk with wine, for that is dissipation, but be filled with the Spirit." (Ephesians 5:18)

God's way of empowering you to live a victorious Christian life is by filling you with the Holy Spirit, moment-by-moment. You will be filled with (directed and empowered by) the Holy Spirit as you:

1. Live by faith.

    "And without faith it is impossible to please Him." (Hebrews 11:6a)

2. Confess and turn away from all known sin.

"If we confess our sins, He is faithful and righteous to forgive us our sins and to cleanse us from all unrighteousness." (1 John 1:9)

3. Consciously yield each area of your life to God's control.

    "For all who are being led by the Spirit of God, these are sons of God." (Romans 8:14)

ILLUSTRATION:_____.

TIMOTHY'S WEEKLY SPIRITUAL GROWTH ASSIGNMENT:

A. Continue your daily Quiet Times using your *Spiritual Journal* and the Quiet Time Reading Guide. Be prepared to share your insights next week.

B. Take sermon notes using your *Spiritual Journal*. Be prepared to share your highlights next week.

C. Continue reading the Gospel of John at your own pace.

SESSION SEVEN DISCUSSION GUIDE

7

DISCUSS LAST WEEK'S ASSIGNMENTS

BUILDING A CHRISTIAN CHARACTER

The more Scripture we treasure in our hearts, the easier it is for the Holy Spirit to *guide* and *protect* us.

A. Scripture Memory helps us resist _____ and live in _____.

> *"How can a young man keep his way pure? By keeping it according to Thy word."* (Psalm 119:9)

If you fill your _____ with sinful thoughts, they will eventually influence your _____.

"If you sow a *thought*, you will reap an *action*; if you sow an action, you will reap a *habit;* if you sow a habit, you will reap a *character*; and if you sow a character, you will reap a *life*."

ILLUSTRATION: _____ .

"Above all else, guard your heart, for it is the wellspring of life." (Proverbs 4:23, NIV)

ILLUSTRATION: _____ .

B. Knowing the truth reminds us of the _____
of sin.

"Be not deceived; God is not mocked: for whatsoever a man soweth, that shall he also reap." (Galatians 6:7, KJV)

"But put on the Lord Jesus Christ, and make no provision for the flesh." (Romans 13:14, NKJV)

ILLUSTRATION: _____ .

C. Scripture Memory channels your thoughts in a _____
direction.

"Finally, brethren, whatever is true, whatever is honorable, whatever is right, whatever is pure, whatever is lovely, whatever is of good repute, if there is any excellence and if anything worthy of praise, let your mind dwell on these things." (Philippians 4:8)

D. Scripture Memory provides help when you_____
_____!

"Man shall not live by bread alone, but by every word that proceedeth out of the mouth of God." (Matthew 4:4b, KJV)

E. Scripture Memory equips you to _____
with others.

Peter said, *"Always be prepared to give an answer to everyone who asks you to give the reason for the hope that you have."* (1 Peter 3:15, NIV)

The writer of Hebrews said, *"For the word of God is living and active and sharper than any two-edged sword. . ."* (Hebrews 4:12a) The Word of God brings conviction of sin and the awareness of Christ to the hearts of unbelievers.

F. It provides direction for making wise daily_____.

"Thy word is a lamp to my feet, and a light to my path." (Psalm 119:105)

We should make our decisions in light of Biblical principles.

HOW CAN I INTERNALIZE GOD'S WORD?

A. Build the Bible into _____.

B. Learn the _____.

C. Utilize natural _____.

    1.   Learn phrases one at a time, adding them as you go.

    2.   Meditate on the meaning of each phrase.

D. Repeat the reference before and after each verse .

Think of the reference as an integral part of the verse itself.

E. Review for _____.

One of the easiest ways to review is to _____ new verses with your friends *". . . iron sharpens iron."* (Proverbs 27:17b)

F. Meditate for _____.

Filling your mind and heart with Scripture will greatly increase the quality of your fellowship with God.

David said *". . . I remember Thee on my bed. I meditate on Thee in the night. . ."* (Psalm 63:6)

"How blessed is the man who does not walk in the counsel of the wicked . . . but his delight is in the law of the Lord, and in His law he meditates day and night." (Psalm 1:1 & 2)

THE CHALLENGE TO BUILD A GODLY LIFE!

Paul said, *". . . discipline yourself for the purpose of godliness."* (1 Timothy 4:7b)

"But flee from these things, you man of God; and pursue righteousness, godliness, faith, love, perseverance and gentleness." (1 Timothy 6:11)

". . . Let us throw off everything that hinders and the sin that so easily entangles, and let us run with perseverance the race marked out for us. Let us fix our eyes on Jesus, the author and perfecter of our faith, who for the joy set before Him endured the cross, scorning its shame, and sat down at the right hand of the throne of God." (Hebrews 12:1 & 2, NIV)

A CALL TO FAITHFULNESS!

". . . If you abide in My word, then you are truly disciples of Mine." (John 8:31)

- Continue to enjoy daily Quiet Times using your Quiet Time Reading Guide.

- Memorize Psalm 119:11 for personal growth.

- Keep witnessing to others about Christ.

- Continue reading the Bible at your own pace.

- Enjoy journaling, worship, and prayer.

Congratulations upon completing *A Call To Joy*! We sincerely hope that you will continue the spiritual growth process so you will keep maturing in Christ!

A CALL TO GROWTH

This highly practical series includes eleven sessions teaching:

- The *five* most basic aspects of prayer.

- The "hows" and "whys" of independent Bible study.

- How to share your faith naturally using *three* different lifestyle methods:

  1. **A Word of Truth**
  2. **A Personal Testimony**
  3. **"The Bridge Illustration"**

- Principles for dealing with *temptation*.

- The joy of *giving* to the Lord with a grateful heart.

- Keys to continued personal growth.

"For I am confident of this very thing, that He who began a good work in you will perfect it until the day of Christ Jesus."
(Philippians 1:6)

INSPIRATIONAL READING

Chapters
1 – 5

CHAPTER 1

THE LOVE
OF GOD

"Yet to all who received Him, to those who believed in His name, He gave the right to become children of God." (John 1:12, NIV)

Congratulations for indicating your desire to make Jesus Christ the Lord of your life. This is the most rewarding and important decision you will ever make!

During the next few weeks, it will be my privilege to assist you as you learn how to grow in your personal relationship with God. To begin with, let's review what you did when you invited Christ to be your Savior. You may have done this recently, or at some time in the past. But you now desire to grow in spiritual maturity.

Let's start reviewing what the Scripture teaches in John 1:12. If after reading this passage you still lack assurance that you have received Christ, a prayer is provided on page 43. Praying this prayer with faith and understanding will enable you to personally settle this matter in your heart.

GOD'S LOVE

The depth of God's love for us is revealed in the fact that He wants us to become His very own children. Everyone in the world was created by God, and *each one of us shares the same heavenly invitation to become far more than His creation.* God wants us to be His children, members of His family.

To explain this invitation, the Bible focuses on two important words of action: *believe* and *receive.* Pretend you have a glass of water in your hand. You are hot, thirsty, and nearly dehydrated. You believe the water is cool and good, but it cannot quench your thirst until you drink it – until your parched body receives it. *Believing without receiving is not enough!* But believing is the beginning.

God designed our physical bodies to need water, and He uniquely created water to meet that physical need. The spiritual principle of life is exactly the same. We needed to know God, and God sent His Son, Jesus Christ, into the world to meet that spiritual need. When we receive Christ into our hearts, we come to know our heavenly Father. Through this unique relationship, He provides all the love, forgiveness, and guidance we will ever need. He quenches our thirst for His presence. His well will never run dry. Another parallel between physical reality and spiritual reality can be seen in architecture. No superstructure is ever built without first laying a foundation. This is universally true. In 1 Corinthians 3:11, Paul says, *". . .no man can lay a foundation other than the one which is laid which is Christ Jesus."* You must believe enough in the Lord's power to change you, receive Him by faith, and let Him establish that spiritual foundation in your life.

BEGINNING A NEW LIFE

Years ago, in Anchorage, Alaska, I taught these verses during a conference on spiritual growth. A young woman who had attended every session seemed to be unhappy; there was no radiance in her smile. She didn't laugh when others laughed, or take part in the activities. Toward the close of the week, as I taught on salvation, she began to cry. Soon, she made her way to the front of the auditorium. I asked if she understood what I had been saying. She said that she had not understood anything for four nights, but when John 1:12 on *believing* and *receiving* was explained, she saw her spiritual condition.

I explained that *once you realize your need for forgiveness, there are two steps to salvation. The first is intellectual acceptance. The second is your willingness to receive Christ by faith.* I said, "He is a gentleman and will not force His way into your life. He knocks and wants to come in, but you must offer the invitation." She had never understood this before.

She told me that she lived in an apartment about three blocks from the church, but had never attended services. She had been living in adultery with a man for a long time. The week before, he had left a note simply saying, "I'm leaving, you'll never see me again." At the age of 23, she had a baby but no marriage, a past but no future, a present but no happiness. She read the note and threw herself on the bed. She prayed, "O, God, I haven't talked to You for years, but if You are there, if You are real, please answer me. I have made a terrible mess of my life and I need Your help. I need forgiveness. I want to live differently."

Here was a young woman who had been to church not more than three times in her entire life. She had no relationship with God, but was now sincerely seeking Him. In the quietness of her heart, God impressed her to leave her apartment and enter the first church building she saw. He let her know that the help she needed was waiting there. By God's providence, that was where I was leading a conference on spiritual growth.

When she entered the church building, she saw books and a registration table. She paid the conference fee, thinking that must be what it cost to go to church. Because ten churches were participating in the meeting, everyone assumed that she was a member of a congregation other than their own and no one suspected her need. But she persevered and sat alone every night.

One evening, I went through the plan of salvation, illustrating how we were created by God, but had been separated from Him by sin. I explained the wonderful news: that through believing in Christ and receiving Him, one could become a child of God. As the Holy Spirit opened her eyes, for the first time in her life she saw the importance of receiving Christ.

Her new life began with a prayer like this: *"Lord, I believe in You and want You to be my Savior. Please come into my heart and take control of my life. I have sinned and need Your love and forgiveness."* Her overwhelming joy was evident as she gave thanks that her prayer had been answered. Through the Lord Jesus Christ, she was born into God's kingdom and became one of His very own children.

Today, many people do not understand that intellectual belief in God is not enough. They are surprised to learn that the Scriptures say that even the demons believe in one God, but that doesn't get them into heaven. Personal commitment is required for salvation. That is why the act of *receiving* Christ is so important.

LIVING WITH ASSURANCE

After laying the spiritual foundation of *believing* and *receiving*, what comes next? In 1 John 5:13, the Bible says, *"These things I have written to you who believe in the name of the Son of God, in order that you may know that you have eternal life."* The word *"know"* stands out as the emphasis of this verse. As His children, God wants us to be assured of His love, faithfulness, and supreme adequacy to see us through both this life and the next. In His love, He chose to let us *know* rather than guess or only hope about the reality of our salvation. God does not intend for us to wait through life to find out if we are going to heaven. First John was written so that God's children might have that certainty.

In Romans 8:16, the apostle Paul says, *"And the Spirit Himself bears witness with our spirit that we are children of God."* It is God who reminds you that you are His child. With each passing year, your assurance and understanding of that reality will grow. Though remembering the exact hour or day when you received Christ is desirable, it is not necessary. However, knowing that there was such a time is essential. Billy Graham's wife, Ruth, reared on the mission field in China, came to faith at an early age. When asked about her conversion, she once replied, "I'm not sure when the sun came up, but I'm certain that it's shining!" This certainty is the birthright of every person who receives Christ into his life.

I well remember my own conversion. I was only ten years old and alone in my room. Though I vividly recall making the decision, I cannot remember the date. But I will never forget the joy that filled my heart when I awakened my parents and said, "Mother and Dad, I have become a Christian." I knew what had happened! Although I had only prayed the single word, "yes," God knew all that it implied. In later years, I have often thought of the simple prayer of the repentant thief on the cross who said, *"Lord, remem-*

ber me when You come into Your kingdom." (Luke 23:42, NKJV) That was not a wordy request, but it was enough to make the difference for eternity, because God knew he meant it.

God looks into our hearts. What we mean by what we say is far more important to Him than the way we say it. The sincere prayer of the smallest child is as pleasing and acceptable to Him as the petition of the most mature adult. If you have the inner peace that comes from the assurance that you have already sincerely invited Christ into your heart, reading the pages that follow will significantly deepen the quality of your relationship with Him.

However, if your life still has no spiritual foundation, and you lack the assurance that you have received Christ into your life, you have *nothing to fear.* God has promised to honor the desires of your heart (Psalm 37:4 & 5). Though you may have believed in Christ with your mind, you now realize your need to personally receive Him into your life. He is prepared to answer your petition.

Prayers of sincere repentance based upon Jesus' famous parable about the prodigal son (Luke 15:11-32) have been expressed to God by millions across the centuries. Here is a prayer that includes what the Lord taught in that parable. It is called "A Prayer for Salvation." If you still feel a need to be certain of your own relationship with Christ, pray this prayer in faith.

There is no magic in the particular words of this prayer, for *receiving Christ is an act of the will. Your prayer simply reflects the inward decision you are making.* Have you trusted Christ completely for forgiveness and guidance? If not, this moment and your earnest commitment will make the difference in how and where you spend eternity.

If you have been *hoping* that you are a Christian, but want to know for *certain*, God wants you to have that *assurance.* Why not pause now and quietly talk with Him? Consider each thought in this prayer and express it to God in your own personal way.

A PRAYER FOR SALVATION

"Lord Jesus, I am a sinner. But I am sorry for my sins. I want to turn from my sins. I am willing to begin a new life with Your help. Lord Jesus, please come into my heart and life right now. From this moment forward, my life belongs to You and You alone. I will love You, serve You, tell others about You, and trust You to live Your life through me. Thank You Lord, for coming into my life and for forgiving my sins today."

What have you just done? You have received the Lord Jesus Christ as your personal Savior! Because of this, there is great joy in heaven. You might be saying to yourself, "This is wonderful! But what should I do next?" For salvation, you have made the all-important step of receiving Christ by faith. Now you must learn how to walk in Him.

CHAPTER 2

LEARNING TO WALK

"As you therefore have received Christ Jesus the Lord, so walk in Him." (Colossians 2:6)

Learning how to walk in Christ is your next step in Christian growth. In this step, you will discover the joy of telling others about your decision to follow Christ. The Lord said, *"Whoever acknowledges Me before men, I will also acknowledge him before My Father in heaven."* (Matthew 10:32, NIV) What does that mean? Simply this: When you love someone, it is natural to talk about them. You want others to know about the close friendship you share. *The Lord wants no secret disciples, and when you love Him, you will want to be baptized, join a church fellowship, and begin to witness where you work or go to school. These things will come naturally as you grow.*

Before a person learns how to walk, he must learn to crawl. Walking and maturing are part of this process. There is no single moment when you suddenly become mature. It is the same in your spiritual pilgrimage: birth (receiving Christ) comes first. Then comes crawling, walking, and finally running. This involves wonderful years of growing in fellowship with God. The apostle Paul

45

speaks of Christian maturity as running the race and finishing the course (1 Corinthians 9:24, 2 Timothy 4:7).

Walking requires energy, and just as we gain physical strength through eating, we need to nourish ourselves spiritually as well. In 1 Peter 2:2, the apostle says, *"Like newborn babes, long for the pure milk of the word, that by it you may grow..."* When you were born, the first thing you needed was nourishment. A child needs milk. You don't have to instruct him to want it – the desire is natural. There is an excitement and beautiful satisfaction when that need is met. *On a spiritual level, the desire to know God's Word corresponds to a baby's natural hunger. For this reason, the Word of God is often referred to as spiritual food.*

How do you feed yourself spiritually as you learn to walk in Christ? God has equipped us with five senses. One of these senses is the ability to hear. The Bible says, *"Faith comes from what is preached, and what is preached comes from the word of Christ."* (Romans 10:17, JB) Every time you attend a Bible study or go to church, you have the opportunity to hear the Word of God. Each time you listen, you are given new spiritual truths. This is God's way of increasing our faith. Jesus said, *". . . Man shall not live by bread alone, but by every word that proceeds from the mouth of God."* (Matthew 4:4, NKJV) *The Bible itself is our source of spiritual nourishment.*

Listening is a primary means of spiritual growth; however, there is an unexpected hurdle which we must all overcome. *Scientists have proven that we forget approximately 90 to 95 percent of what we hear after 72 hours. If you heard your favorite preacher or could even listen to the apostle Paul, you would still forget about 90 percent of what he said after three days. The truth is, most of us cannot remember much from last Sunday's sermon. This is not because of a lack of dedication. Our problem is retention!* Unless what we hear meets a very specific need in our lives, we simply cannot remember it.

So note-taking is important. It compensates for our human tendency to forget; it encourages those who preach and teach from the Scripture, and it helps us meditate on what we hear, so we can apply God's Word in our lives.

I discovered the value of note-taking after several years of frustration. As a teenager, I publicly rededicated my life nine times. I guess the people at our church must have thought I had a lot of problems. In reality, what I was trying to say was that I wanted to grow deeper in my commitment to Christ. It was not that I had become less dedicated. I simply didn't know how to retain the blessings I was receiving. Perhaps you have had a similar experience. Unfortunately, there was no place on the commitment card which said, "I want to be a man or woman whom God can use, and I need someone to teach me."

Learning how to listen will be essential to your spiritual growth, and note-taking will help you succeed. Most teachers have the tendency to slow down, make their points clearer, and even repeat them when they see someone is taking notes.

WHERE TO TAKE SERMON NOTES

It is appropriate to take notes on God's Word at every opportunity. However, even this small discipline requires a little planning. Taking notes on scraps of paper, bulletin inserts, and offering envelopes will not result in the kind of growth which you are seeking. For this reason, the *Spiritual Journal* with a helpful note-taking section has been developed.

The use of this Journal will help keep you from the experience of my good friend, a West Texas cattleman, who was at a Bible conference in Houston. A wonderful British Bible teacher was exhorting us from the Scriptures. As we walked across the street together, I asked him, "How is God speaking to you through this conference?" This man, who was in his seventies and wore a Stetson hat, cowboy boots, and a western suit, said, "Son, my cup is full and running over." That was his explanation of how greatly he was being blessed. About six weeks later, I ran into him in another city. When I asked, "How is your cup?" he pensively replied, "Had a hole in it."

Perhaps you have had the same experience. You went to a conference, church service, or a crusade, and you were greatly blessed, only to discover a few days later that you felt empty again. Remember, your problem may not be a lack of dedication, but simply a lack of retention.

WHY TAKE SERMON NOTES?

Some Christians live the first year of their Christian lives over many times. Instead of growing, they end up on a treadmill, learning and forgetting the same lessons year after year. The object of spiritual growth is not to live the first year nine times, but to live nine progressive years of the Christian life!

According to a national survey, the average minister spends twenty hours per week in sermon preparation. When he realizes that Sunday after Sunday, his average church member will retain only three minutes of content from a thirty-minute sermon, it has to be discouraging. If you want to encourage your pastor, let him know that you are serious about listening. When you meet him at the door instead of saying, "I enjoyed the service," mention one specific verse, insight, or illustration that helped you. Tell him how God used the sermon to positively affect your life. Through this, he will know that you heard what the Holy Spirit was saying through the message.

Practical application is retention's best friend. When your actions and attitudes are positively affected, your recall will increase as well. Science has demonstrated that you remember 90 percent of what you hear, read, and then do. Your spiritual objective should therefore focus on James 1:22 (NIV), which says, *"Do not merely listen to the word, and so deceive yourselves. Do what it says."* Your first practical step toward victory is simply beginning a lifestyle of taking good notes.

The objective of note-taking is not to outline the sermon or the Bible study lesson. What matters is recording what the Holy Spirit is teaching you personally as you listen to the Word of God. Write down the things that will make a difference in your life, insights you can actually apply. The test of good listening and good application is life itself. When you leave church or a Bible study, you need to go out better prepared to live positively and effectively.

REVERENCE FOR SCRIPTURE

Spiritual growth occurs when we meditate upon what God says and then apply it in our daily lives. Because this is true, we need to cultivate an attitude like the people of Ezra's day. They hungered for a Word from God! Nehemiah 8:2-6 says: *"And Ezra, the priest,*

*brought the Law before the congregation, and he read therein from
morning until mid-day, and the ears of the people were attentive.
And when he read, all the people stood up, and Ezra blessed the
Lord, the great God, and all the people answered, 'Amen, Amen.'"*
(Paraphrased)

Why did they stand up? Wouldn't they have been more com-
fortable sitting down? Yes. But they stood up out of respect for
God's Word. Can you imagine such a congregation? Can you believe that they chose to stand up all that time?

Today, it's hard to get people to come to listen, even in air-
conditioned comfort. But to Ezra's congregation, inconvenience
didn't matter.

"When Ezra read, all the people stood up. . ." These words
took on a fresh meaning for me several years ago. I was once in an
African congregation that stood every time the Bible was read. The
respect that the congregation held for the Scriptures convinced me
that too many of us do not value the sacredness of God's Word.

In recent years, some countries have been blessed with an amazing array of up-to-date translations which include a wide assort-
ment of chain references, concordances, and other helpful information. *With all these modern blessings, you must carefully guard
against taking your Bible for granted. The privilege of reading its
sacred pages is still beyond the reach of a large percentage of the
world's population.* Only in the light of this overwhelming truth
can we begin to appreciate the value of its availability.

The scarcity of Bibles in other countries was vividly brought to
my attention several years ago as counselors were being trained for
an evangelistic campaign in a West African country. Although Christians had been in the area for decades, the nation was largely made
up of animists (those who still hold ancient pagan beliefs about
multiple gods and spirits, usually active in nature). Being unfamil-
iar with many of their country's unique problems, I wrote ahead to
organize the crusade in a routine manner. Our standard Bible study
requirements caused the counselors in training to walk for miles,
sometimes barefooted, to join a friend who owned a prized possession – a Bible. Months later, when I arrived to preach, my heart
was deeply moved when I realized how insensitive we had been due
to our Western assumption that every Christian had a Bible.

In Ezra's day, the problem was even more pronounced. People
had to gather to hear and listen to God's Word from the handwritten
scrolls which had been painstakingly copied.

CARRYING YOUR BIBLE

Owning a Bible is a privilege, and carrying it with you is a witness in itself. Spurgeon, a famous British Christian, used to say, "Carry your Bible with you every place you go, because it will preach a thousand sermons a day!" How true this is. When people see your Bible, they automatically think of its message; and the Holy Spirit will apply conviction, comfort, or hope to their hearts.

As a student, I learned this valuable lesson. One day in class, my Bible toppled off my other books and landed on the floor. My agnostic teacher immediately stopped the class, saying, "Billie, your Bible has fallen on the floor." Though she had never received Christ as her Savior, her deep respect for what He stood for caused her to spontaneously honor His words of truth. This simple occurrence provided a natural opportunity for me to talk with her privately. I explained that if the Bible were already meaningful to her, its inspired message would affect her even more when she came to know its Author. Though she was much older and also my teacher, it was obvious from the look in her eyes that she received that suggestion with genuine appreciation.

A GODLY ATTITUDE

You will increase your joy in reading the Bible and hearing its message preached and taught if you learn an important secret.

In Memphis, Tennessee, I have a friend who was invited to be a guest speaker in a church which is known for its long services. After an hour of congregational singing and testimonies, a beautiful piano solo was played. A lady stood up in the back of the congregation and reverently said, "Yes, Lord, yes." Time passed, and another person stood and said the same thing. After several minutes, a large percentage of the congregation had stood to their feet and said, "Yes, Lord, yes."

My friend was perplexed because he had not heard a question. Finally his host, a well-known pastor looked heavenward and said, "Father, we have given You our response in advance. Now speak to us through Your messenger and tell us what it is You desire for us to do." *The secret to joy and worship is listening with a prepared heart. What God is looking for in every Christian's attitude is faith expressed in a pre-determined will to obey.*

Have you ever attended a church service when the last thing you felt like doing was worshiping the Lord? We need to guard our frame of mind and worship with a spirit of expectancy. This requires planning ahead, because invariably the whole world seems to clamor for our attention immediately prior to the worship service. What a difference it will make in your life when you come to church saying, "Yes, Lord, yes." When this is the attitude of your heart, God will begin to use your life in wonderful new ways!

Too many of us listen to God's Word as if we were partaking of a smorgasbord. We want to select a little bit of this and a little bit of that from the Bible, but we do not come with a pre-determined will to receive whatever God says we need and then apply it in our lives. All too often, our attitude is something like this: "Lord, I want to hear what You have to say to me as long as it fits what I already plan to do." The net result is that we ask Him to bless what we want to be blessed. We try to ignore what we do not want to hear. Mature worship is putting ourselves under the authority of Jesus Christ by saying, "Yes, Lord, yes. I'm available; I'm willing; I'm eager to do what You want me to do."

Having believed in Christ and having received Him as your Savior, your love for Him will be evidenced by listening to His Word and walking in obedience to His will. *Because He came to give you an abundant life, His leadership will always direct you to the highest plain of fulfillment.* We have His unfailing promise: *"I will instruct you and teach you in the way which you should go; I will counsel you with My eye upon you."* (Psalm 32:8)

Using the note-taking section of the *Spiritual Journal*, will you commit yourself to the Lord to grow in your faith by taking notes on what you hear from the Bible?

_____ Yes
_____ No

"Faith comes from what is preached, and what is preached comes from the word of Christ." (Romans 10:17, JB)

CHAPTER 3

THE PERFECT EXAMPLE

"Very early in the morning, while it was still dark, Jesus got up, left the house and went off to a solitary place, where He prayed." (Mark 1:35, NIV)

The Lord's perfect life is an example for all mankind to follow. The world has had many teachers, but only one Christ – His actions were as inspired as the words which He spoke.

THE EXAMPLE OF JESUS

He started His day with the Father, not only because He wanted to, but because in His humanity He actually needed to. Each time He departed for a season alone in prayer and personal fellowship with the Father, His human needs were met. Beyond that, He was showing His disciples how to live victoriously. He arose early on this particular morning (Mark 1:35) and chose to be totally alone. On the day before, He had preached in Capernaum, freed a man possessed by demons, healed Peter's mother-in-law, and preached again to a huge crowd where great numbers of spiritually, physically, and emotionally sick people were healed (Mark 1:21-34). It is an understatement to say that His schedule had been busy.

Everyone wanted to be with Him – the sick and disturbed, new followers, disciples in training, and hangers-on; they were all pressing in upon Him. To get any time alone with the Father, Jesus literally had to get up while it was still dark and slip away while the others were sleeping.

This devotional practice was essential in the Lord's earthly life because He lived in dependence upon the spiritual strength given to Him by His Father. He carefully reminded His disciples that no work He did was of Himself, and that no word He ever spoke was His own. He credited the Father with everything accomplished in His ministry (John 14:10). He literally lived each moment in dependence upon His Father. Ironically, our Savior who spoke only of dependence, was seen by the Jewish leaders of the day as the most independent man they had ever met (Mark 1:27).

During the Lord's solitary times of prayer, He was sometimes interrupted. Such was the case on this particular morning; *"And Simon and his companions hunted for Him; and they found Him, and said to Him, 'Everyone is looking for You.'"* (Mark 1:36 & 37) Several important lessons can be seen in this experience, but first concentrate on the person of Christ. What really happened when He was interrupted? Visualize the Lord talking to His Father. Consider the fact that He was filled with the Holy Spirit without measure (John 3:34). Allow the exalted meaning of this verse to permeate your mind; *"For in Him* (Christ) *all the fulness of Deity dwells in bodily form."* (Colossians 2:9) Everything that God is, was present in the life of Christ. Since prayer is a conversation, one could accurately say that Peter and the other apostles unknowingly interrupted a holy time of communion among God the Father, God the Son, and God the Holy Spirit. To be sure, this was a most holy moment.

When the Lord's prayer time was interrupted, He demonstrated what our reaction should be. He did not chide those who intruded upon His time with the Father. He did not allow the interruption to upset His spirit or ruin His day.

His lifestyle remained consistent yet flexible, regardless of the outward circumstances. But how does this relate to us today?

PRACTICAL DEVOTIONS

The Lord Jesus and the early Christians lived in that pre-electric era when people normally went to bed early and got up early. If they wanted to do anything at night, they had to build a fire or use a small oil-burning lantern. Although Jesus rose early, it was probably after getting a good night's rest. *The point of this passage is not to rise before the sun comes up, but rather to start your day with God whenever your day normally begins.* This principle will hold true for shift workers, night watchmen, and people of every vocation.

No specific hour is established in the Bible for your daily Quiet Time. You do not have to be like the famous British cricketer, C. T. Studd, who is said to have read the Bible by candlelight in the early morning hours. I will never forget the guilt trip I went on once after hearing a marvelous sermon on the Quiet Time. After that service, I thought the only way to be spiritual was to get up at 4:00 a.m. and read the Bible by candlelight! *The key to spiritual growth is not how early, but how expectantly and consistently one meets with the Father.*

Medical science has discovered that all of us have a biological clock. Our bodies actually require differing amounts of sleep in order to work at peak efficiency. I have a good friend from Africa who only needs four or five hours of sleep per night, but most people need seven or eight.

Alexander the Great had a very unusual biological clock. It is said that when needed, he could sleep 72 hours and work 72 hours. This was one of the ways he won his battles. He wore out one army after another! No one else could concentrate on the fight that long. He learned to use his strengths and limitations, and when he died at the age of 32, he had already accomplished a great deal. It is important to get to know your own sleep requirements, so you can plan ahead to be wide awake for your Quiet Times. Eventually in your Christian experience, no matter how dedicated you are, you will face the reality of fatigue. The Lord faced it. One afternoon He went to sleep in a boat (Matthew 8:23-27) and demonstrated to His disciples that when exhausted, the most spiritual thing you can do is rest!

Relating this principle to your own Quiet Time, remember that trying to keep one eye open while reading the Bible is like attempting to talk to someone when you are only half awake. Under normal circumstances, if a person who really loves you sees that you are exhausted, he will want you to go ahead and sleep. God's attitude is clearly revealed in the Scripture when He says, *"He gives His beloved sleep."* (Psalm 127:2b, NKJV)

GETTING STARTED

Let me challenge you to join the countless millions whose lives have been changed by beginning their day with a Quiet Time. Ten to fifteen minutes each morning will make an amazing difference in your day. Why not stop right now and dedicate these "special minutes" to God. Give Him the beginnings of all your future days. Ask Him to continually remind you of the important commitment you are making. As you pray, thank Him for the high privilege of spending time alone in His presence.

All spiritual growth is based upon decisions. The choice you are making to begin a daily Quiet Time is one you will never regret. Through it, you will grow in fellowship with God and in your ability to minister to your fellow man.

Every journey starts with a first step, and a Quiet Time begins by simply waking up and getting out of bed in the morning! I am reminded of the story about a man who always stayed in bed while trying to read the Bible. One day he confessed that "Something came up," and he missed his Quiet Time. His confession was overheard by his guardian angel who candidly remarked, "Something came up, indeed! It was big and white, and looked exactly like a sheet!"

The opposite side of fatigue is oversleeping. Some people are "spendaholics." They spend God's money on this, that, and the other, and then they have nothing left to give. Others are "workaholics." They work, work, work, until no time is left to be with God because they have substituted activity for worship.

Then there is the "sleepaholic." If you are a sleepaholic, let me suggest that you memorize Proverbs 6:9, which says, *"How long will you lie down, O sluggard? When will you arise from your sleep?"* When you commit that verse to memory, the Holy Spirit will use it time after time to awaken you when you are rolling from one side of your bed to the other in the morning. I can assure you this is true, because He has used this verse with me on more than one occasion.

"I overslept" is perhaps the most commonly used excuse for not having a Quiet Time. Over the years, as I have taught on this

subject, approximately 15 percent of the conferees have said that they are very sluggish in the mornings, 15 percent have said they wake up bright and eager to begin the day. Another 70 percent say they get up reasonably well, but they still have trouble being alert. A Quiet Time is intended to be *fun*, so let me give you a few practical suggestions on this matter of being awake and alert. While some of these suggestions are more serious than others, all of them can be helpful.

Analyze what gets you awake in the morning. For my wife, it is coffee. She frequently drinks it before or during her Quiet Time. For men, let me recommend Mennen's Skin Bracer. Don't drink it – just splash it on your face, neck, elbows, and kneecaps, and you will feel like running around the room. It's tremendous! For the same effect, ladies can use Charles of the Ritz Tingling Astringent.

Exercise is also good. Recently in Korea, a veteran missionary showed me his tried and proven method. He shakes his hands vigorously while running in place for one thousand steps. This is followed by an ice cold shower! In favorable climates, a brisk morning walk before Bible reading will accomplish the same objective. The Scripture says, *"discipline yourself for the purpose of godliness"* (1 Timothy 4:7b), so whatever approach you use, make up your mind in advance to carry it through.

For those who have a particular aversion to mid-winter devotions, I have heard of one unique wake-up approach. If you sleep on the right-hand side of the bed, put your right leg out of the covers first. If you do not get up immediately, just let it hang off the edge of the bed and it will grow uncomfortable after a while. Soon you will swing your left leg over to join it. Before you know it, you will be up washing your face and getting ready for the day!

Remember this thought: even though the Scripture says, *"Be still, and know that I am God"* (Psalm 46:10a, KJV), let me suggest that you not be too still. The objective is to get out of bed to read and pray. If you do not, your Quiet Time will inevitably be too quiet!

EVENING DEVOTIONS

There are several hazards in having your devotions at night. I am not saying that God will not bless it, but it often amounts to giving Him the "leftovers" of your day. You are already tired. You have given your best to the world, your job, and the people around you. But the One who deserves the most receives the least. Make note of four hazards related to having your devotions at night: energy spent, pillow soft, lights dim, print small! I have experienced every one of these hazards and have unintentionally fallen off to sleep.

As a young Christian, I attempted to have my Quiet Time at night simply because I didn't know any better. Like so many people, I would sleep until the last minute and rush to class in the mornings. For years, my only Scripture reading and prayer was at night. My grandmother had given me a large Bible. One evening as I was reading it, the pillow seemed so soft and the light looked so dim that I soon fell asleep with the Bible on my chest. I didn't move until the next morning. While the Bible was on my chest, in the zone between sleep and wakefulness, I kept subconsciously thinking, "Something is wrong!" The Bible's weight produced a strange feeling. I remember opening my eyes very slowly and seeing the words "Holy Bible" upside down. A sentimental feeling swept over me: "I slept all night with a Bible on my chest!" There's one thing you can be sure of – that's not the way to increase your spirituality!

Charlie Riggs of the Billy Graham team has said, "The Word of God has to get into your mind, and then make an 18-inch trip down into your heart." How true that is. *You have to be alert enough to think through what you are reading if it is going to affect the way you live.*

When I heard about the value of having a Quiet Time, I accepted a six-week challenge to begin spending ten minutes each morning with God. It was like eating honey – once you taste it, you want more. The Psalmist said, *"How sweet are Thy words to my taste! Yes, sweeter than honey to my mouth!"* (Psalm 119:103) As time passed, I came to understand the testimony of Jeremiah: *"...Thy words became for me a joy and the delight of my heart..."* (Jeremiah 15:16)

You can begin your day with God and end it with Him as well. If you want to read and pray at night, that's great, as long as it is not your only Quiet Time. Enjoy your spiritual cake in the morning, and the icing before you go to sleep at night!

CHAPTER 4

THE SECRET
OF GODLINESS

"Discipline yourself for the purpose of godliness." (1 Timothy 4:7b)

No one reaches godliness by accident. It is only as you seek personal purity, determine to be holy, and allow Christ to be in control that the victorious Christian life becomes experientially yours. Spiritual growth, unlike physical growth, is the product of personal commitment. We decide to discipline ourselves for the "purpose of godliness." As we make Christ-honoring decisions, He gives us all the power we need to live them out.

This new life is one which the secular world cannot fully understand. Paul describes its uniqueness in 2 Corinthians 5:17, *"Therefore if any man is in Christ, he is a new creature; the old things passed away; behold, new things have come."* Paul's personal testimony reflects his complete change in values. *"Whatever things were gain to me, those I have counted as loss. . ."* But why? *". . . In view of the surpassing value of knowing Christ Jesus my Lord. . ."* (Philippians 3:7 & 8a) *Christians have a new and different mindset.* The Scripture says, *"If you have been raised up with*

Christ, . . . Set your mind on the things above, not on the things that are on earth." (Colossians 3:1a, 2)

The new thoughts, actions, and deep affections that come with receiving Christ are nurtured by our close fellowship with Him. Like most new disciples, the first verse I ever learned was John 3:16, *"For God so loved the world, that He gave His only begotten Son, that whoever believes in Him should not perish, but have eternal life."* Years later, a friend showed me 1 Corinthians 1:9 and explained its wonderful meaning. It became my second memory verse: *"God is utterly dependable, and it is He who has called you into fellowship with His Son Jesus Christ, our Lord."* (PH) It was through this passage I discovered that every Christian has a calling – yes, a high calling to have fellowship with Christ.

GOD DESIRES OUR FELLOWSHIP

Why set aside a Quiet Time for prayer and daily Bible reading? Because God Himself is faithfully calling us into a life of fellowship with His Son. To disappoint that holy desire on the part of God for even one day would be a tragedy. In John 4:23, His desire for fellowship is emphasized by Jesus: *"An hour is coming. . .when the true worshipers shall worship the Father in spirit and truth; for such people the Father seeks to be His worshipers."* Fellowship, our highest calling, is at the very heart of our worship and everything else we do as God's children. Through it, we are participants in His highest purpose for life.

The daily Quiet Time is not a program designed by men, nor is it a legalistic ritual based on tradition. It is the outward response of our innate desire to truly know God. Listen to the words of the apostle Paul after having been a Christian for many years. The hunger of his heart was to deepen that fellowship: *"That I may know Him, and the power of His resurrection, and the fellowship of His sufferings. . ."* (Philippians 3:10a) Paul wanted to know every aspect of having a close relationship with his Creator.

Love is like that. Married couples will quickly testify that after having known and loved each other for years, they are still learning to appreciate new aspects of one another's personalities. Love is spelled T-I-M-E. To really know someone requires years of fellowship in a wide variety of circumstances. This same rule applies to your walk with God.

THE REASSURANCE OF HIS LOVE

Hunger for God is as old as man himself, but few have expressed this longing with the clarity of Moses. In his beautiful prayer he says, *"O satisfy us in the morning with Thy steadfast love that we may rejoice and be glad all of our days."* (Psalm 90:14, Paraphrased) He grasped an essential truth about God's love: It is steadfast, unchanging, and secure.

Morning by morning Moses had experienced the secret of joy and gladness. He was walking in close fellowship with the God he loved in spite of all the difficulties the world could hurl in his direction. Put yourself in his place: at the age of 80, he was responsible for moving 600,000 men and their families to the country of Canaan (Exodus 12:37). The hostile Egyptian army was behind him, a burning desert lay in front of him, and he had very little food and water. Humanly speaking, he had nothing but problems. In addition to all these obstacles, the people were unhappy most of the time. He bore the heaviest kind of responsibility in the worst kind of working environment. It was in this setting that he learned the supreme value of spending his mornings with God.

Wouldn't you like to be inwardly satisfied at the dawning of each new day? Think about a delicious meal that satisfies your hunger, or a drink that satisfies your thirst. *The daily Quiet Time is designed to satisfy your hunger for God Himself.* If you have responsibilities, live in a challenging environment, or need to be reminded that God loves you, the same joy that Moses experienced is ready and available.

If Christians cannot live as proof of an abundant, positive joy, who in this world can? The person in your mirror has a right to be happy! You have been redeemed and are now God's child. You are free to live out your potential to the fullest extent. Ephesians 2:10 says, *"For we are His workmanship, created in Christ Jesus for good works, which God prepared beforehand, that we should walk in them."* You are a special person with a special mission. Each and every morning, God wants to remind you of who you are in Christ.

OUR NEED FOR DIRECTION

Psalm 143:8 is one of many practical verses in the Bible. It deals specifically with having a daily Quiet Time. David says, *"Cause me to hear Thy lovingkindness in the morning, for in Thee do I trust: cause me to know the way wherein I should walk; for I lift up my soul unto Thee."* (KJV) If there was ever a man in the Bible who needed to have a daily Quiet Time for guidance, it was David. When he says, *"I lift up my soul unto Thee,"* it literally means, "I place my life in Your hands."

Consider David, a man whose life was lived in constant conflict – a man's man, fearless and decisive. Why did he pray for direction and help? Because he grasped the reality of his own need. As a shepherd boy, David learned to trust God when protecting his flock from dangerous animals. While still a teenager, he faced the giant soldier, Goliath, with only a sling. As a young man, he spent years running from King Saul, who had once been his friend. He lived in danger from the Philistines throughout adulthood. In later life, two of his own children (Absalom and Adonijah) sought to take his throne by violence. Though he lived in crisis, David became a man after God's own heart (1 Samuel 13:14), a man God deeply loved. Even when he sank to the very depths of sin (2 Samuel 11), he rebounded and received the forgiveness for which he longed. He prayed daily for practical direction, for he had tasted failure and he was well aware of his need.

Perhaps the best wisdom is learning from the mistakes of others and not making them yourself. Failing that, at least we can learn from our own poor choices and not repeat the same sin over and over again. *Someone said that we Christians all learn to pray eventually: the question is whether we will be praying for guidance, or forgiveness.* To re-state an old maxim, an ounce of guidance is worth more than a pound of forgiveness.

As a new Christian, I learned this lesson in the school of hard knocks. It seemed that every night my prayers would begin the same way: "Lord, forgive me for all my sins." Unfortunately, my list never included my failure to seek His guidance. The sin of presumptuousness is subtle but real, and it leaves millions of Christians living in mediocrity. *God wants us to go into the day with the benefit of His counsel, but all too often we end our day in needless defeat, simply because we have neglected to seek His direction.* God's guidance is as generously available as His forgiveness. He says, *"I will instruct you and teach you in the way which you should go; I will counsel you with My eye upon you."* (Psalm 32:8)

DRY SPELLS

No matter how much you love the Lord or the depth of your dedication, there will be times of spiritual dryness in your life. Usually these will merely be the result of physical fatigue. On other occasions, they may be the result of boredom, unresolved conflicts, medical difficulties, or unconfessed sin. David suffered acutely from middle-aged boredom, and Moses chafed under the unending ingratitude of those to whom he ministered. No one is exempt from times of spiritual dryness. Though these periods are not desirable, God can use them to teach you valuable lessons. It is often as a result of these occasions that you can most clearly see His faithfulness.

How can dry times be avoided? Consistency is the key! A good athlete does not work out only when he feels like it. He trains daily, because he knows that exercise is in his best interest and will make the difference in winning or losing to his competition. The same is true with farming or any other worthwhile activity. The Bible says, *"Let us not become weary in doing good, for at the proper time we will reap a harvest if we do not give up."* (Galatians 6:9, NIV)

Let's assume that you make a spiritual commitment to keep growing, but miss your Quiet Time for some good reason. The devil will try to turn that perfectly legitimate situation into the beginning of a dry spell. His tactics will probably operate something like this: he'll say, "If you really were a dedicated Christian, you would have gotten up this morning and had your Quiet Time. You made a commitment to spend time with God, and this morning you didn't do it." He will carefully avoid the fact that you stayed up late the night before doing something important which was spiritually on target. If you are in the will of God staying up late, you can also be in the will of God sleeping late! You need to memorize this verse: *"There is therefore now no condemnation for those who are in Christ Jesus."* (Romans 8:1) Satan does not have the right to condemn you as a Christian, because you do not belong to him. You are God's child.

Have you ever given your neighbor's child a spanking? It is a hazardous venture, because only your most discerning friends will appreciate and affirm your helping them with discipline. Many people would be offended by it. By and large, we spank our own children because they are our own responsibility. In the same way, the Bible says, *"God chastises those whom He loves."* (Hebrews 12:6a, Paraphrased) God gives us our spiritual spankings because we are His and He loves us. Satan has no right to administer correction, condemnation, or anything else to you as a Christian; so be careful not to let him discourage you as you walk with Christ.

A seminary professor once shared a principle which has been extremely helpful to me over the years. He taught me that "God convicts in specifics...and Satan condemns in generalities." For example, if you missed several Quiet Times for poor reasons, Satan might say, "Jim, you just don't have what it takes to be dedicated. To be honest, I don't think you are going to make it. If you really loved God, you'd do better." Satan will try to condemn you and make you feel defeated. Count on it. It's predictable!

In contrast, the Holy Spirit might say something like this, "Jim, you are My child and I love you, but you missed a real blessing this morning. I had something special to share with you from My Word. Be careful not to keep missing these times together, because you will not receive a blessing if you're not there."

God will always call attention to your omission, and He will also convict you about the need to correct the problem, but He will never condemn you for committing the sin. Satan will condemn you as a person because he wants to erode your self-worth. In contrast, God will convict you about the sinfulness of an act, but at the same time He will continually affirm you as a person and build your self-worth.

Failing to understand this basic difference has caused many people to get the activities of God and Satan mixed up. God operates out of concern with man's best interest at heart, but Satan plays by a different set of game rules. His desire is to weaken your witness and to entice you into an undisciplined lifestyle of spiritual compromise. He uses condemnation as a tool to achieve his purpose. He wants you to be negative about yourself, your friends, the church, the Bible, and if possible – even about life itself. His objective is to get you discouraged so you will quit trying to grow.

Be smart and remember that the enemy has no power over you whatsoever unless you give it to him of your own free will. *"There is therefore now no condemnation for those who are in Christ Jesus."* (Romans 8:1) We fight a defeated enemy, and *"We are more than conquerors through Him who loved us."* (Romans 8:37b, NIV) The secret of achieving godliness can be found in a lifestyle of spiritual consistency. The matchless life which has been made possible through Christ's death and suffering is already ours potentially, and it becomes ours experientially as we choose it on a day-to-day basis. What kind of life do you really want? This is the issue. Everything required for your happiness has already been provided. You are free as God's child to live a life of incomparable victory! The Scriptures declare, *"I press on toward the goal for the prize of the upward call of God in Christ Jesus."* (Philippians 3:14)

CHAPTER 5

PRINCIPLES FOR LIVING IN VICTORY

"But in all these things we overwhelmingly conquer through Him who loved us." (Romans 8:37)

PRINCIPLE #1: Growth Comes Slowly

"And let endurance have its perfect result, that you may be perfect and complete, lacking in nothing." (James 1:4)

As newlyweds, my wife and I had the unique experience of being houseguests of the Billy Grahams on Christmas Day. My spiritual dad, Grady Wilson, and Billy Graham, his lifelong friend, decided to play golf that afternoon. In order not to reveal my poor golf game, I quickly volunteered to be Dr. Graham's caddy. He had recently had surgery and seemed pleased with the suggestion. As we covered the mountainous North Carolina course, I took every opportunity to ask questions. Once when he sliced the ball, I said something like, "Life is sometimes like that, isn't it?" to which he replied, "Yes, some go off to the left, and others to the right." He described how those who move to either extreme diminish their own capacity for letting God use them in life.

We walked and talked, and I asked him if there were still many verses in the Bible that gave him trouble. He said there were some which he had been praying to understand for over twenty-five years. He went on to express an amazing truth – that when you really need to understand a passage, "God opens it up and it blossoms like a beautiful flower. In His own time, He reveals the hidden meaning and beauty of each facet of His Word."

Jesus illustrated this truth in His model prayer (Matthew 6:9-13). He taught us to pray in an attitude of patience. He didn't say, "Give us this day our full week's bread in advance." We were told to trust Him for one day at a time. Spiritually speaking, daily bread is God's only means of provision. When the Lord called Himself the *"bread of life"* (John 6:35), He sought to deepen our understanding of the reality that our daily bread is spiritual as well as physical. He said, *"Man does not live on bread alone, but on every word that comes from the mouth of God."* (Matthew 4:4b, NIV)

For most of us, eating is enjoyable. On the average, we eat about a thousand meals each year. The physical changes produced by eating take place so slowly that from one day to the next they cannot be seen. But our bodies are never static. Each day we change. Remember the impatience of childhood? Next year seemed an eternity away. Only as we mature do we come to understand that both spiritual and physical growth come slowly.

PRINCIPLE #2: Use Common Sense

Old-fashioned common sense is a virtue which will help insure a life of spiritual victory. For fun, imagine I am walking down a street in your town and you see tears streaming down my cheeks. Concerned, you ask, "Billie, why are you crying? You look so sad!" Forlornly I reply, "I missed lunch!" I say, "I made a commitment years ago to be an eater. I promised to be consistent! But today I blew it; I missed lunch. I just don't have what it takes. I'm through; I'll never eat again."

If you miss a meal, you simply compensate for it later. You do not stop eating. If you miss your daily Quiet Time, the same principle applies. Simply have a longer prayer time and more Bible reading later. This could be that night, or even the next morning.

There is nothing legalistic about eating your favorite meal. Why?

Because eating is a pleasure. Just as your physical hunger reminds you to visit the refrigerator, your spiritual hunger reminds you to read the Bible. *Self-imposed starvation and malnutrition are as foolish spiritually as they are physically, so use common sense and feed yourself.*

PRINCIPLE #3: Guard Your Affections

Some time ago, I was talking with a fellow minister about the importance of Christ being first place in our lives. Matthew 6:33 says, *"Seek ye first the kingdom of God . . ."* (KJV) I asked, "What do you think this verse really means?" I will never forget his answer. He said, "Billie, Christ doesn't mean first place in a traditional sense. What if you went home to your wife and said, 'I want you to know how much I love you. You are first place in my life. However, I want you to know about Mary Lou, Jane, Rose, and Jeanette. They are in second, third, fourth, and fifth place!'" I got the point. Do you think my wife would be happy just being in first place? Not at all. A wife or husband wants to be your only sweetheart, not just the first one on the list.

This is the spirit of Matthew 6:33. Christ wants to be first, and He wants to be all. His call to discipleship is always clear and always has been. He said, *"Unless you love Me more than your father, your mother, your wife, and your own life also, you cannot be My disciple."* (Luke 14:26, Paraphrased) This was not a new teaching but an echo of the first commandment, *"Love the Lord your God with all your heart and with all your soul and with all your mind."* (Matthew 22:37, NIV) As we learn to love God with all that we are, He can begin to love others through us. Because He lives in us, there is an inexhaustible supply of love available for us to share with those close to us, and those around the world. In his parting challenge in the Upper Room, He reminded His disciples of His new commandment: *"...love one another, even as I have loved you..."* (John 13:34)

Spiritual victory is achieved by allowing God to re-order our priorities and affections. In Colossians 3:2, Paul instructed us with these words, *"Set your mind on the things above, not on the things that are on earth."* If you want to find out if Christ is in first place, examine three areas of your life: your thoughts, your time, and your giving.

YOUR THOUGHTS

What do you enjoy thinking about? In Philippians 2:5, you are challenged to *"Let this mind be in you, which was also in Christ Jesus."* (KJV) The text goes on to say that the Lord humbled Himself to become a servant. Do you enjoy thinking of new ways to serve Him? In Philippians 4:8, the Bible says, *"Finally, brethren, whatever is true, whatever is honorable, whatever is right, whatever is pure, whatever is lovely, whatever is of good repute, if there is any excellence and if anything worthy of praise, let your mind dwell on these things."* Your mind is a mirror of your affections. When you truly seek His kingdom, you will know it. Your own thoughts will reveal it.

The Scriptures teach us this important principle: As a man *"thinks within himself, so he is."* (Proverbs 23:7a) We become like the things we think about. For this reason, the Bible says, *"Above all else, guard your heart, for it is the wellspring of life."* (Proverbs 4:23, NIV) You may be asking, "How do I guard my heart?" When the Bible refers to the heart, it is usually a reference to that part of your mind where life's deepest decisions are made. This is also the place where your affections are formed. *In a spiritual sense, you are guarding your heart when you guard your mind. It is a matter of both mental and spiritual hygiene.*

The Scripture warns, *"If anyone loves the world, the love of the Father is not in him."* (1 John 2:15b) This teaching is easy to understand in light of the First Commandment, *"Love the Lord your God with all your heart."* (Mark 12:30a) As a person gives his love to God, he has less left for the sinful things in the world around him.

YOUR TIME

Do you enjoy being with God in times of fellowship, recreation, worship, and training? The first Christians completely reordered their lives. They left everything they had to spend every possible hour with the Master. In those periods together, He taught them how to be *"fishers of men."* Mark 3:14a says, *"And He appointed twelve, that they might be with Him ... "* Their great service to the world followed the time spent in His presence.

Though the radical nature of the apostles' calling in most cases will not resemble the specific way God deals with you, the spirit of your calling is the same as Peter's, James', and John's. To them, their time with Christ was so valuable that they climbed mountains and walked the long, winding, dusty roads of Judea and Galilee to be near Him. (Matthew 17:1)

It is sobering to think that some Christians who look forward to heaven, will not rise fifteen minutes early or attend services on Sunday to be with Him here on earth. I have often wondered what it is people expect to experience in heaven that makes them think they want to go there. If they do not cherish the music of praise and the fellowship of His children, or love to hear the eternal truths of His Word, how strange the surroundings of heaven will seem.

The apostle John, describing that future time says, *"And I heard, as it were, the voice of a great multitude. . . as the sound of mighty peals of thunder, saying, 'Hallelujah! For the Lord our God, the Almighty, reigns.'"* (Revelation 19:6) Every moment spent praising Him and getting to know Him at the deepest human level is time that will have eternal value, because your relationship with Him will last forever. If you find yourself too busy for that kind of fellowship, you are too busy!

YOUR GIVING

"Where your treasure is, there will your heart be also." (Luke 12:34) *If you want to know what is important to you, look at your checkbook stubs.* Most of us are afraid to do that because we do not want to face the truth. They would show that our highest motivation and true goal for making money is not really the Great Commission. Our affections are still earthbound. We may suspect this and sometimes even grow a little concerned about it, but God cannot use us mightily, nor trust us as He would like to, until the "Goliath of ownership" has been slain in our lives.

As your daily Quiet Time becomes consistent and you begin to understand the principles on which God operates, you will discover that giving is at the very heart of His nature. Your personal spiritual growth can be measured by the answer to this question: "How much am I becoming like Him?" As you are conformed to His image, your new attitude will resemble that of David's day: *". . . the people rejoiced because they had offered so willingly, for they made their offering to the Lord with a whole heart."* (1 Chronicles 29:9)

Soon this will dawn on you: every moment of your life, every possession you value, every friendship you hold dear, every accomplishment you have achieved have come to you only through God's love. When this dawning occurs, you will be overwhelmed! You will be gripped with the desire to give back to Him in return. Did He not give you the mind, the will, and the strength to make everything you do and have possible?

The psalmist says, *"The earth is the Lord's, and all it contains, the world, and those who dwell in it."* (Psalm 24:1) Christ owns the 100 percent; yet He generously gives us 90 percent to invest, enjoy, and live on. The tithe, 10 percent of our income, is all that He requires, but a Christian's most joyful giving is often done well beyond that minimum. Why? Because of the knowledge that these funds will be used to help fulfill the Great Commission and bring the Good News of Jesus Christ to every nation of the world (Matthew 28:19; Matthew 24:14).

In Chapter 29 of First Chronicles, you will discover a fact which has always struck me as humorous, even though David expressed these thoughts in sincere worship and praise. In verse 12 he says, *"Both riches and honor come from Thee. . ."* and then, *"who am I and who are my people that we should be able to offer as generously as this? For all things come from Thee, and from Thy hand we have given Thee."* (verse 14)

The only thing we have to give God is what He has already given us. This is why we can never overgive or outgive God. One of my close friends says, "When we give to God, He is also giving to us. He just uses a bigger shovel!"

One Father's Day, I had an experience which brought this message home. My ten-year-old, Heather, decided to go shopping. For two years she had saved the money we had given her for making good grades. When I walked through the door, there were house slippers, pajamas, a robe, a new shirt, a tie (not a tie I would have picked, but a modern tie she thought I needed), and a shaving kit. The shaving kit contained soap, perfume, shaving lotion, and just about everything you could want. She was standing there beaming with delight! I picked her up, hugged her, and thanked her from the bottom of my heart. Then I asked, "Honey, how much did you spend?" (a typical father's question). The reply was, "Everything I had." I thought to myself, *"How impractically wonderful!"*

Love is like that. Do you think I would ever knowingly let

Heather go broke or suffer for having given me everything she had? Obviously, as her father, I have the power to give her back what she gave me many times over. What thrills me is the fact that she did the giving on her own, and that she did all she could. That, I will never forget.

So the deepest truth about giving is that both the 10 percent and the 90 percent are actually His. Everything you are is His. When your unrighteousness was exchanged for His goodness (2 Corinthians 5:21), the title deed of your life was passed to God forever (1 Corinthians 6:19). Your physical body became His earthly temple. You were no longer your own, for you had been bought with a price (1 Corinthians 6:20). From that point forward, you were treated as His very own child. When you try to shower Him with your love and your gifts, though they may seem large to you, they are never more than a small fraction of what He has already given. Why does God rejoice in our giving? Not because He needs it, but because He wants to see us become like Him. And He – is a giver! *"For God so loved the world that He gave. . ."* (John 3:16)

PRINCIPLE #4: CARVE ISLANDS IN YOUR DAY

"But the news about Him was spreading even farther, and great multitudes were gathering to hear Him and to be healed of their sicknesses. But He Himself would often slip away to the wilderness and pray." (Luke 5:15 & 16) The news about Christ was spreading. His ministry was growing and His responsibilities were increasing. When the pressures of life begin to build, we are presented with two options. We can either control our circumstances, or we can allow them to control us. The Lord Jesus modeled the right decision.

Paradoxically, the more you have to do, the less time you have to do it in. Recently I had lunch with a famous Bible teacher who is in much demand throughout the world. He said "Billie, I have a tremendous frustration in my life because this year I have received 2,000 invitations to speak. It is hard for me to know which of them the Holy Spirit intends for me to accept." As the impact of his ministry has increased, his need for wisdom and guidance has increased in direct proportion.

We have already discussed the importance of beginning your day with God. However, the Lord not only started His day in prayer, but as one busy businessman has put it, He "carved islands in His day." At every opportunity, He would slip away to be with the Father.

Even on the most noted day of His public ministry, Jesus planned ahead to have an island of time alone. Having fed 5,000 men and their families with only five loaves and two fish, He spoke to the multitudes ". . . *teaching them many things.*" (Mark 6:34, NIV) It was late in the day when the disciples picked up twelve baskets of broken pieces of bread and fish. Immediately, the Scripture says, ". . . *He made His disciples get into the boat and go ahead of Him to the other side (of the Sea of Galilee) to Bethsaida, while He Himself was sending the multitude away. And after bidding them farewell, He departed to the mountain to pray.*" (Mark 6:45 & 46)

Jesus broke all precedent on this occasion. Normally, He would have dismissed the multitude and taken the twelve to some quiet spot where they could talk together about His teachings. On this occasion however, He purposely separated Himself from the twelve. The only way for Him to be alone was to plan His day and make the circumstances compatible with His will. Because the twelve always pressed for His time and attention, He sent them away in order to have seasons alone with the Father. After dismissing the multitude, He carried through with His plan to have a Quiet Time. He went up on the mountain and spent the evening in prayer. He was in control of His life.

Mark wrote, *"And when it was evening, the boat was in the midst of the sea, and He was alone on the land. And seeing them straining at the oars, for the wind was against them, at about the fourth watch of the night, He came to them, walking on the sea; and He intended to pass by them."* (Mark 6:47 & 48) We are all familiar with the miracle of His walking on the water as He crossed the Sea of Galilee, but have you ever stopped to consider the reason He did it? Every activity of that late afternoon and night was calculated to serve His purpose. He did not walk on water as a public miracle to be gazed at. He even intended to pass His own disciples by. The one and only reason this miracle was necessary, was the supreme importance He attached to being alone in prayer. You and I cannot walk on water to have a Quiet Time, but we can make provision for being alone with God as Jesus did.

How can we follow His example in today's world? For starters, we can cut the radio off in the car and use travel time for prayer and meditation. We can listen to cassettes of the Bible while walking or jogging, call a moratorium on excessive TV viewing, and create an atmosphere of quiet in our lives. Much of man's noise is a form of escapism by which he attempts to fill his loneliness. For the Christian, islands of quiet are times for listening, planning, fellowship, and peace of mind.

The great decisions of Jesus were normally made during these private times. His twelve apostles were chosen after a full night of prayer (Luke 6:12). And the greatest victory of His life was accomplished in solitary agony as He prayed, *"Not what I will, but what You will."* (Mark 14:32-36, NKJV) If it had not been for the triumph at Gethsemane, there would have been no Calvary.

Ultimately, the forgiveness of our sins was made possible as the result of Jesus' unfailing commitment to carve islands in His day for prayer. It was through this practice that He lived in unbroken obedience and perfect fellowship with the Father. That same provision is available for each one of us. James says, *"If any of you lacks wisdom, let him ask of God, who gives to all men generously. . ."* (James 1:5a) If we fail to take advantage of this provision, it is simply an evidence that we *"have not because we ask not."* (James 4:2b, KJV)

Who will suffer if we fail to carve islands in our day? If Jesus had failed, He would have forfeited His destiny, but we would have been the ones to suffer. The same concept holds true today. *If we fail to listen, we forfeit our ministry, but those we could have reached for Christ will pay the greatest price for our spiritual indifference.*

PRINCIPLE #5: Put Others First

The Scripture says, *"Do for others what you want them to do for you."* (Matthew 7:12, LB) With this Golden Rule in mind, let's pose a question: *what if you were depending upon someone like you to explain the plan of salvation to you? What would be the likelihood of your learning how to go to heaven?* Would you want their prayer life of intercession on your behalf to be like yours? Would you want their discipline and knowledge of the Bible to resemble yours? How about their love? Would you want their level of concern for your eternal destiny to be equated with the burden you have for others?

If your honest answers to these questions are "No," then you will understand why God wants to produce major changes in the quality of your life. People mattered to Jesus. For this reason, He strove to be everything they needed. He said, *"I have come not to be ministered unto but to minister."* (Mark 10:45, Paraphrased) He reminded us that a student is not above his teacher (Matthew 10:24a). He showed us how to bear witness at every turn in life by reaching down to the defeated like the woman at the well (John 4:4-26), and challenging intellectuals like Nicodemus (John 3:1-15). We are called to do the same.

If you were a greedy swindler like Zacchaeus (Luke 19), a leader like Lazarus (John 11), a man of wealth like Joseph of Arimathea (Matthew 27:57), a rebel like Paul (Acts 8), a common fisherman like Peter (Matthew 4:18), a timid teenager like John Mark (Acts 13:13), an immoral woman like Mary Magdalene (Luke 8:2), or a tender woman of faith like Mary of Bethany (John 11), – how would you want to be treated? Would you want someone to share the Gospel of Christ with you?

As we look at the several billion who populate our world, and consider the small percentage who have received Christ as their Lord and Savior, this question becomes extremely personal. Put yourself in their position—confused, lonely, or even bitter. At best, they have a very limited understanding of what God might be like. Living without Christ, their minds are focused on things that are material. Paul says, *". . . those who live as their human nature tells them to, have their minds controlled by what nature (flesh) wants. . ."* (Romans 8:5a, Good News) This results in spiritual death.

Jesus said, *"I came that they might have life, and might have it abundantly."* (John 10:10b) Because people were His purpose for coming to earth, as He lives through us, they will become our purpose as well. The apostle Paul explains how we learn to put people first when he declares, *"For it is God who is at work in you, both to will and to work for His good pleasure."* (Philippians 2:13)

If you want to live in victory, the ultimate means for this adventure is Christ Himself. No list of principles, however true they may be, will insure the quality of life which you desire. But be assured that victory is yours for the taking, because the One who lives in you is victorious. Rely upon Him to live out His resurrected life – *through* you. He is more than adequate for every trial and opportunity in your future. As you review these five principles, decide to let Him live them out through you on a daily basis.

QUIET TIME
READINGS

1 – 30

QUIET TIME 1

How can you *know* for certain that you are a Christian and that you have eternal life?

Let's look at 1 John 5:11-13. *". . . God has given us eternal life, and this* *life is in His Son. He who has the Son has life; he who does not have the Son of God does not have life. I write these things to you who believe in the name of the Son of God so that you may know that you have eternal life."* (NIV)

Because God loves you, He wants you to enjoy a life filled with inner peace and confidence! He has given you His promise of eternal life from the very moment of your conversion until – forever. That's the good news proclaimed in the Bible.

Christ's death and resurrection have made it possible for you to be in a right relationship with God, both now and forever. The Bible calls this relationship eternal life. Because you received Jesus Christ as your Lord and Savior, you can *know* that you will be a part of God's family throughout eternity!

This assurance is not based upon your feelings, but upon God's promise. The Bible says, *"Yet to all who received Him, to those who believed in His name, He gave the right to become children of God."* (John 1:12, NIV)

Scriptural Insight	*Prayer*
I can be confident that I have eternal life because of God's promises in the Bible.	*Father, thank You for making me a Christian and giving me eternal life.*

QUIET TIME 2

How was your salvation made possible?

The apostle Paul gave the answer to this question: *"For by grace you have been saved through faith, and that not of yourselves; it is the gift of God, not of works, lest anyone should boast."* (Ephesians 2:8 & 9, NKJV)

These verses clearly explain how you were saved, so read them again and circle the words *"by grace"* and *"not of works."* Think about the meaning of these important words. *"Grace"* literally means the kind of love that is undeserved and can never be earned.

Once a famous Christian was approached by one of the world's wealthiest men. The billionaire said, "I would give anything to have the *peace* you talked about today." The Christian replied, "I am sure that's true, but would you be willing to receive the peace of salvation if it cost you *nothing?"* The wealthy man was perplexed by the question. In daily life he was able to take credit for all his possessions and accomplishments because he had worked for them. The idea of receiving forgiveness as a "gift" from God seemed strange.

It is our pride that makes us want to get to heaven by our own efforts. Solomon, the wisest man in ancient history, was once inspired by God to write these words: *"Pride comes before a fall."* The Bible says salvation can *never* be achieved through works. Why? Because if we ever earned it, we would become proud and boastful!

Let's examine another truth. Since salvation cost the Lord everything, it costs you nothing. But, even if you had been willing to give *everything you had,* still you could not have purchased it! No amount of human effort or wealth would have been enough. Your salvation was a *perfect* gift from a *perfect* donor!

Scriptural Insight	Prayer
My salvation was given to me as a gift. I did not earn it.	Father, thank You for Your grace that enabled me to become a Christian.

79

QUIET TIME 3

What does the Bible teach about the Lord's ability to keep us once we are saved?

Jesus once said, *"My sheep hear My voice, and I know them, and they* *follow Me; and I give eternal life to them, and they shall never perish; and no one shall snatch them out of My hand. My Father, who has given them to Me, is greater than all; and no one is able to snatch them out of the Father's hand."* (John 10:27-29)

Jesus is referring to Christians as sheep. The security of the sheep is not in *their* ability to defend themselves but in their *shepherd's* ability to protect them. God is the only one who is able to keep us secure. We are depending upon His ability, not our own. No one can take you out of your heavenly Father's hand, because He is more powerful than anyone anywhere, and it is He who has given you eternal life!

Assurance comes from knowing that when you become His child, you are His *forever*. To plant this wonderful truth in your mind, imagine that you are holding a coin in the palm of your left hand. Now close your hand, making a fist. Next, grip your left hand with your right hand. Is there any way to drop the coin?

Reread paragraph one. Whose hands are you in? The Bible says you are securely held by both the *Father* and the *Son*.

Scriptural Insight	*Prayer*
I can be confident that I will always be a Christian.	Father, thank You for your power and protection that holds me securely in the palm of Your hand.

QUIET TIME 4

Have you noticed a change in your attitudes since you gave your life to Christ?

 2 Corinthians 5:17 says, *"Therefore, if anyone is in Christ, he is a new creation; the old has gone, the new has come!"* (NIV)

You are *not* the same person you were before you received Christ. Why? Because now, He is showing you the things in life that please Him; and even more important than that, He is causing you to *desire* these new virtues. This is the kind of supernatural change that comes from deep within.

Once a communist who spoke in a city park promised a new *coat* to every listener who would embrace his political doctrine. At the close of the speech, a Christian asked for equal time. He countered the offer by promising that God would put a new *man* in every coat if they would repent of their sins and place their faith in Jesus Christ!

The world is primarily interested in new and better coats, but God is interested in new and better men!

In the New Testament, when the hated tax collector, Zacchaeus, became Christ's disciple, he returned to the same house in the same clothes on the same day, but he was a new man. The inner change had taken place. A new life had begun!

The Christian message is always *good news*. When a person decides he really wants to change, what a joy it is to learn that God has already provided a way!

Scriptural Insight	Prayer
You have made me into a new creation because I have received You into my life.	*Father, thank You for the change you have made in me since becoming a Christian.*

QUIET TIME 5

How does work fit into the process of spiritual growth? If salvation is a gift from God, what is my responsibility?

The apostle Paul once wrote, *"And let us not lose heart in doing good, for in due time we shall reap if we do not grow weary."* (Galatians 6:9)

Being tired because of energy expended in doing good is to be expected. The Lord Himself was weary on many occasions, but being tired of *doing good* is *not* an acceptable option for a Christian. We are called to follow His example of consistent service. He said, *"...he who believes in Me, the works that I do he will do also..."* (John 14:12b, NKJV)

Once a high-society crowd in formal dress eagerly awaited a performance by the famous composer and pianist, Ignace Jan Paderewski. A small boy, restless with waiting, slipped away from his parents, went to the stage and began playing "Chopsticks" on the grand piano. Hearing the angry roar that rose from the audience, Paderewski hurried to the stage unannounced. He leaned over the boy and began to play a beautiful counter melody which harmonized with the simple tune. As he played, he whispered in the boy's ear, "You're doing good. Keep on playing – don't quit."

Your first efforts in serving the Lord may seem simple and faltering, but you can rest assured that your willingness will be crowned with success if you faithfully continue.

This is the summarized message we have from God: Don't stop! If misunderstood, do good; if unappreciated, do good; if tired from years of service, keep doing good! Don't cease doing My work in the world!

Scriptural Insight	Prayer
Now that I am a Christian, I want to find some way to serve God out of love.	Father, please show me some way that I can be of help at our church.

82

QUIET TIME 6

Why attend church?

Hebrews 10:24 & 25a says, *". . . and let us consider how to stimulate one another to love and good deeds, not forsaking our own assembling together, as is the habit of some, but encouraging one another..."*

When Christians come together for worship, we *share* our strength, faith, and understanding. It is in this fellowship that we seek to grow in the likeness of Christ. Church is not a *place* – it is a group of forgiven people who are attempting to carry out God's plan for their lives.

Encouragement – What a powerful word. It is the essence of brotherly love. Christians are called to meet together for the purpose of stimulating one another to *"love and good deeds."* We need to be supportive when problems come and affirm the importance of each other's strengths and abilities.

The giant redwood trees on the West Coast of the United States are among the oldest and largest trees in the world. Many of them have stood for centuries against the onslaughts of nature, but what is the secret of their great strength? It is not the depth of their roots – in fact, they have a very shallow root system for their size. The answer is hidden in the fact that these mammoth trees stand close enough together for their roots to intertwine. This *bond* of unity gives them the ability to stand against the most violent storms.

The amazing endurance of the church, in spite of tremendous persecution, testifies to the importance of studying God's Word, praying, singing, laughing, and even crying together!

Scriptural Insight	*Prayer*
It is very important for me to attend church.	*Father, thank You for the people at my church and for the help they have been to me.*

QUIET TIME 7

What does the Bible teach us about time management?

 "And the whole city had gathered at the door. And He healed many who were ill. . . [and the next day,] in the early morning, while it was still dark, He arose and went out and departed to a lonely place, and was praying there." (Mark 1:33, 34a, 35)

It was after a very busy day of serving that Jesus got up early to spend time alone with His heavenly Father. When you face hectic days, reflect on His example. Notice that He lived according to a set of *priorities* that were out of step with the rest of the world. *Every activity,* even activities *for* God, had to take second place to His time alone *with* God.

What would happen if you decided to live like that? You would enjoy the uncommon qualities of peace, certainty, and wisdom that characterize those who prioritize their time the way He did.

In the New Testament, a lady named Martha once worked hard serving as the Lord's hostess, while her sister Mary sat at His feet and listened to His teachings. Why did Jesus compliment Mary, saying she had *"chosen the good part?"* (Luke 10:42b) Because she valued *time* with Him in the same way that He valued *time* with His Father.

To be truly effective in Christian service, you must learn how to *distinguish* between the *good* and the *best.* Even worthwhile activities will begin taking second place to your time alone with God. The further you go, the more you will desire to devote yourself to Bible reading and prayer.

Scriptural Insight	*Prayer*
I need to always make it a priority to spend time with God every morning.	*Father, help me to be disciplined and consistent to spend time with You each morning so I can keep growing spiritually.*

QUIET TIME 8

What happens if I sin now that I am saved?

 First, it is important to remember that the Lord's death on the cross was more than adequate to pay for any sin you have committed, or ever will commit. Second, God's Word says that He loves us and wants us to enjoy an *abundant life* on a daily basis. This is why He wants us to bring sins to Him the moment they occur. 1 John 1:9 says, *"If we confess our sins, He is faithful and just to forgive us our sins and to cleanse us from all unrighteousness."* (NKJV)

What does it mean to *confess* your sins? It means to *agree* with God in prayer about any attitude, motive, or action that displeases Him. When you sincerely seek to *renounce* your sin, He stands ready to forgive and cleanse you. Through this continual cleansing, your fellowship with God will stay fresh, and you will experience the full *joy of your salvation.*

God will not only *forgive* our sin when we honestly confess it, but will also *cleanse* and *purify* our hearts. This is His promise!

The following are five types of prayers that you may wish to consider when writing your prayer each morning:

Petition: "Lord, help me to. . ."
Thanksgiving: "Lord, thank you for. . ."
Adoration: "Lord, you are. . ."
Confession: "Lord, please forgive me for. . ."
Intercession: "Lord, please help. . ."

Scriptural Insight	*Prayer*

QUIET TIME 9

What if God wants me to do something, but I feel I'm unable?

The apostle Paul said, *"I can do all things through Christ who strengthens me."* (Philippians 4:13, NKJV)

The adequacy of Christ is assured to every one of His disciples. He said, *"In the world you will have tribulation; but be of good cheer, I have overcome the world."* (John 16:33b, NKJV) When God leads you to attempt something which seems impossible; this is merely His way of helping you mature in your faith.

The Lord will *never* call you to carry out a task unless *He* is already committed to doing it *through you.* In Christ, you are never limited to your own resources.

After a devastating tornado ripped through a Texas town, an extraordinary photograph appeared on the front page of the newspaper. It showed a piece of straw deeply imbedded in a telephone pole! Under normal circumstances, this could never have happened, but when impelled by the mighty power of a tornado, the fragile straw accomplished the impossible!

You will sometimes stand in amazement as the Lord begins to strengthen you. Once you were too timid, too weak, or too defeated to serve Him, but now you are a chosen vessel – called to a life of victory!

Scriptural Insight	*Prayer*

QUIET TIME 10

How can I start serving God in small ways?

Words are *important!* Proverbs 15:1 says, *"A gentle answer turns away wrath, but a harsh word stirs up anger."* (NIV) What we say can either accomplish great *good* or do great *harm.*

When was the last time you hurt someone by something you said? Do you remember the emotion and pain which you felt later as you considered your unkind words? The Bible says, *"For every species of beasts and birds, of reptiles and creatures of the sea, is tamed, and has been tamed by the human race. But no one can tame the tongue..."* (James 3:7 & 8a)

Consider the testimony of Isaiah 50:4: *"The Lord God has given Me the tongue of disciples, that I may know how to sustain the weary one with a word."*

What a privilege it is to speak when a word is needed! No one can fully estimate the positive impact a single comment can make when spoken at just the right time.

As a boy, one of North America's best-known authors was plagued by low self-esteem. One day in class, his essay was returned with these words written across the top of the page – Henry Wadsworth Longfellow! Those three words of encouragement symbolized a challenge which became the driving force behind his life.

Scriptural Insight	*Prayer*

QUIET TIME 11

Do you remember facing a temptation you felt you could not resist? Have you ever wondered if other people were tempted in the same way?

Paul answers that question: *"No temptation has overtaken you but such as is common to man; and God is faithful, who will not allow you to be tempted beyond what you are able, but with the temptation will provide the way of escape also, that you may be able to endure it."* (1 Corinthians 10:13)

The Bible says quite clearly that you *will face temptation*. Being a Christian doesn't alter that, but it does change the way you will react when tempted. Keep in mind that there is a great difference between temptation and sin. To be *tempted* is *not* a sin. Temptation is being lured to do something that is not God's will. Sin is the willful decision to yield to that temptation.

This verse contains three facts to remember when you are tempted. *First*, you are *not alone* in your battle. *Second,* God will *not allow* you to be tempted beyond your ability to resist. *Third,* God *always* provides a *"way of escape"* when you are under attack. No temptation is irresistible. The question is, "Are you *willing* to take the way out?"

Philippians 4:13 says, *"I can do all things through Christ . . . "* This includes choosing the right path when it is difficult. Each time a temptation presents itself, the first thing to look for is the "exit." When you are *willing*, all the power you need will be there to back up your right decision!

Scriptural Insight	*Prayer*

QUIET TIME 12

What well-known pitfalls should I look out for on my spiritual journey?

 In a self-centered world, you will constantly be tempted to draw attention to yourself. When the apostle Paul preached in the city of Corinth, he faced a similar temptation, so he consciously planned to uplift Christ and not himself. This is why he wrote, *". . . I determined to know nothing among you except Jesus Christ, and Him crucified."* (1 Corinthians 2:2)

This concept was beautifully illustrated when a veteran missionary once visited friends in Thailand. A magnificent orchid was displayed in the center of the host's dining table. The stunning blossom was often mentioned during the meal. Shortly after leaving the house, the missionary asked the other guests if they could remember the vase used for the centerpiece. No one could! The vase had been totally eclipsed by the *beauty* of the lovely flower.

When you are at your best spiritually, people's *attention* will be drawn to the Lord, not to you. It is the warmth of *His* presence that will linger in their minds.

What impression do you make when you receive recognition or compliments? Does the praise stop with you, or do you sincerely pass it on to Jesus? Remember that your life's mission is to draw the world's attention to Him.

Scriptural Insight	*Prayer*

QUIET TIME 13

"You are the light of the world. . . Let your light shine before men in such a way that they may see your good works, and glorify your Father who is in heaven." (Matthew 5:14a & 16) In the Bible, Christians are called *lights* or *lamps*. Around the world, light has the same purpose – it dispels the darkness!

Once a lady came to her pastor complaining about the factory where she was employed. She wanted to quit working there because nearly all the employees were non-Christians and they constantly used profanity. The pastor listened, then asked her, "Where do you put lights?" Disregarding the question, she complained about their wild parties, drinking, and dirty jokes. Again he asked, "But where do you put lights?"

Puzzled by his response, the lady went on to tell him that some of her associates at work were also involved in immoral relationships. A third time he questioned, "But where do you put lights?" Annoyed she said, "I don't know *where* you put lights. In dark places, I guess!" Suddenly, she realized what he had been trying to say.

The lady's attitude changed when she realized she was called to be the *light of Christ* in that dark situation.

Scriptural Insight	*Prayer*

QUIET TIME 14

". . . you have done well that you shared in my distress . . . For even in Thessalonica you sent aid once and again for my necessities." (Philippians 4:14 & 16, NKJV)

There are *two* important lessons to be learned in these verses. First, as Christians we are to give help to those in distress; and second, as Paul demonstrates, we are to express *gratitude* when we are helped.

One cold winter evening, two seminary students, Nat Spencer and his brother, walked along the banks of Lake Michigan. Suddenly, in the distance, they saw a large steamer begin to sink. Soon The Lady Elgin's 323 passengers were in the freezing waters!

Both Spencer brothers were strong athletes, but Nat was an especially good swimmer. Taking a rope in his hand, the brave student swam to the sinking ship. Fighting the frigid water again and again, he saved the lives of 23 people in this heroic feat; but because of his sacrifice, he spent the rest of his life as an invalid. Would you have expected those whom he rescued to *devote* themselves to meeting his needs? Tragically, he never heard from even *one* of them! Nat did his part, but 23 people *failed* to express their gratitude.

Scriptural Insight	*Prayer*

QUIET TIME 15

"As you therefore have received Christ Jesus the Lord, so walk in Him." (Colossians 2:6)

Initially you received Christ *by faith; continue* in that joy!

Years ago, a little boy begged his father to let him go to the circus which had come to town. After doing his chores, he was given a dollar bill and sent on his way. As he neared the fairgrounds, the circus parade was in progress. When the clown at the end of the parade passed by, the little boy placed his dollar in the clown's hand and went home happily, thinking he had seen the circus. Many Christians live just like this little boy; they mistake the beginning for the end!

The new birth is simply the gateway to a new life. As you learn to *walk by faith,* the world will be filled with wonderful new discoveries. Never become satisfied merely looking back to your conversion. Learn to walk with Him and run with Him. Be assured the best is *always* yet to come.

Paul expressed it this way: *". . . forgetting what lies behind and reaching forward to what lies ahead, I press on toward the goal for the prize of the upward call of God in Christ Jesus."* (Philippians 3:13b & 14) He lived for the future, not the past.

Scriptural Insight	*Prayer*

QUIET TIME 16

Read Psalm 27:11, 31:3, 32:8

The Bible and the indwelling Holy Spirit have been given to every redeemed child of God. Why? So we can *know* and *carry out* His will. Listen to His promise: *"I will instruct you and teach you in the way which you should go; I will counsel you with My eye upon you."* (Psalm 32:8)

God has not put us out to sea without a compass, nor on a journey without a map. To the contrary; we know *who* we are, *why* we are here, and *where* we are going.

The Bible teaches us about the ministry of the Holy Spirit, and it is the Holy Spirit who enables us to understand the Bible. So we need the *combined* help of both to clearly discern God's leading.

We gain knowledge, wisdom, and understanding through reading the Scriptures; but the assurance and inner peace that normally accompany our obedience are the work of the Holy Spirit.

Do you see the *balance?* If you are lopsided and do little Bible reading but spend much time in prayer, or vice versa, it will be more difficult for you to discern God's will.

Scriptural Insight	*Prayer*

Application: J will . . .

QUIET TIME 17

Read Matthew 28:18-20

This was Jesus' final instruction to His disciples before returning to heaven. On the basis of His authority, both they and we were commanded to *"make disciples"* throughout the world.

The apostle Paul's clear awareness of being authorized for service stands out as a vivid example to every Christian. Consider his deep feeling of involvement in this passage: *". . . we are ambassadors for Christ . . . we implore you on Christ's behalf, be reconciled to God."* (2 Corinthians 5:20, NKJV)

You may never be asked to speak on behalf of a president or have the power of a government behind you, but as a Christian, you have a far greater privilege. In your home, your neighborhood, and every other place you influence, you are Christ's representative. Your mission is to call people back to God and make disciples for Jesus Christ.

When a young soldier named Alexander was found to be derelict in his duties, he was brought before Alexander the Great. The powerful king looked at the soldier and said, "Either change your ways or change your name!" When you represent Christ and bear His name, your authority is equaled by your responsibility.

Scriptural Insight	*Prayer*

Application: 𝓙 will . . .

QUIET TIME 18

Read Deuteronomy 6:5-7

We have been called to love God with all our hearts and to faithfully teach our children to do the same. How fortunate we are that this divine mandate is at the same time an invitation to *joy*. It is by keeping this First Commandment that we experience spontaneous happiness!

This is why John could say, "*. . . His commandments are not burdensome.*" (1 John 5:3b) It is never a burden to be asked to do something you truly enjoy. Imagine being asked to smell your favorite flower, eat your favorite dessert, or listen to your favorite music. Would you resist the invitation?

Loving God is sweeter, by far, than any human relationship. Why? Because He *never* misunderstands you, mistreats you, forgets you, or leaves you. He is always kind, merciful, and overflowing with life! He will never embarrass you with impurity or disappoint you by changing His character. He has promised to be consistently holy – to remain the same, "*yesterday, today, and forever.*" (Hebrews 13:8, NKJV)

It is said that respect is the best foundation on which to build a lasting love. With this in mind, consider how *long* and how *deeply* you can love God.

Scriptural Insight	*Prayer*

Application: *I will . . .*

QUIET TIME 19

Read 1 Corinthians 6:19 & 20 three times.

Quietly meditate on the remarkable truth that Christ lives *in* you! *"I have been crucified with Christ; and it is no longer I who live, but Christ lives in me; and the life which I now live in the flesh I live by faith in the Son of God, who loved me, and delivered Himself up for me."* (Galatians 2:20)

Properly understood, the Christian life is not living *for* Christ, but letting Christ live His abundant life *through* you. You are dead. That is to say, the sins which once held you captive have been *"crucified with Christ."* The old, strictly human "you" no longer lives. The life of faith which is now yours comes from His presence *within*. On the outside, you may look the same; but on the inside, new life has been present since the moment you invited Christ to reside in your heart.

The Christian life is not seeking to keep a set of rules to please God, nor is it a philosophy. It is the work of God's Spirit in our lives. This is why unsaved people find the Bible so hard to understand. The Bible says, *"But a natural man does not accept the things of the Spirit of God; for they are foolishness to him . . ."* (1 Corinthians 2:14a)

Living the Christian life without the indwelling power of Christ is impossible. This is why the Bible declares, *"Christ in you, the hope of glory."* (Colossians 1:27) It is the fact that He is *in* you that makes your Christian life a reality.

Scriptural Insight	*Prayer*

Application: J. will . . .

QUIET TIME 20

Read Colossians 1:9-12

Have you ever attempted to pray for someone and not known what they really needed?

Paul's primary prayer request for his fellow Christians was that they might be filled with the knowledge of *God's will*. Why? Because this is what every person needs. Living in God's will is the secret to happiness in this life and the key to a *"Well done, thou good and faithful servant"* in the next!

Intercession focuses on seeking to help align a person with the will of God in a specific area of his life. Beyond this, it brings needs of every kind before the Lord. No subject is too small or too large for intercession; if the problem is of concern to you, it is of concern to your heavenly Father.

The apostle prayed for his fellow believers to receive wisdom and understanding. For the lost he prayed: *"My heart's desire and prayer to God for Israel is that they might be saved."* If you have Christian friends, pray for their spiritual and physical needs. If you have lost friends, ask the Lord to graciously convict them of their sins.

For more than fifty years, George Mueller, who was well-known for his ministry of intercession, prayed for five lost friends. After five years, the first one received Christ. In ten years, two more came to the Savior. Mueller persevered for twenty-five years, and the fourth man was saved. When the fifth man received Christ, the man of prayer was already in the presence of the King! Fifty-two years of intercession had produced its eternal fruit.

Scriptural Insight	*Prayer*

Application: I will . . .

QUIET TIME 21
Read 1 Thessalonians 5:12-18

"Rejoice always; pray without ceasing; in everything give thanks; for this is God's will for you in Christ Jesus." (1 Thessalonians 5:16-18)

How is this possible? As Christians, we can *"rejoice always"* because our joy does not spring from *outward* circumstances, but from the *indwelling* presence of Christ. It is our unique privilege to experience the warmth of divine love and *"peace that passes understanding."* Our *joy* is simply the by-product of this special quality of fellowship with the Father.

The term *"pray without ceasing"* does not mean to actually verbalize your prayers without stopping, but rather to maintain a spirit of prayer that pervades every part of your day. While driving your car, working in the kitchen, mowing the lawn, or exercising, you can enjoy inner dialogue with God and be fully conscious of His presence.

Perhaps you will better understand this concept when you stop to consider the portion of a good conversation that is spent in listening. Prayer is a wonderful two-way conversation in which you can talk to God, and He can talk to you; no one else will ever know what is being said unless you want them to. As the months go by, you will also discover that the better you know Him, the more natural it will be to pray continually.

"Giving thanks in everything" does not mean that we are to thank God *for* every thing that happens to us, but to live in an attitude of faith so we can give thanks *in* every circumstance we experience.

Scriptural Insight	*Prayer*

Application: *I will . . .*

QUIET TIME 22
Read 1 Peter 3:13-15

You have probably already experienced criticism and suffering for one reason or another, but has it been for *"righteousness' sake?"* The Bible says, *". . . to the degree that you share the sufferings of Christ, keep on rejoicing; . . .If you are reviled for the name of Christ, you are blessed, because the Spirit of glory and of God rests upon you."* (1 Peter 4:13a & 14)

When the early Christians were flogged for speaking about the Lord, they went out *"...rejoicing that they had been considered worthy to suffer shame for His name."* (Acts 5:41b)

You will probably be called a "do-gooder," a "holy Joe," and lots of other things when you take a stand for Christ. Jesus predicted this when He said, *"A servant is not above his master."* In His own lifetime, He was called a blasphemer, a glutton, and a demoniac. Why? Because He brought light into darkness, and *". . . everyone who does evil hates the light, and does not come to the light, lest his deeds should be exposed."* (John 3:20)

The Lord said, *"You are the light of the world."* Light is only popular with people who are happy about what they are doing. Stop to consider how much crime, drinking, and immorality occurs under the veil of darkness. It is plain to see why He used this illustration.

Peter has a word for us in 1 Peter 3:17: *"For it is better, if God should will it so, that you suffer for doing what is right rather than for doing what is wrong."* Being persecuted for what you do in the light is a form of suffering which is perfectly *acceptable* for a Christian!

Scriptural Insight	*Prayer*

Application: *I will . . .*

QUIET TIME 23

Read Proverbs 15:16 & 17 three times.

"Better is a little" is a phrase that runs against the current of today's thinking about success!

We forget that Jesus said, *". . . a man's life does not consist in the abundance of his possessions."* (Luke 12:15b, NIV) In the early church, few Christians came from the ranks of nobility, wealth, or status. It was the common people who heard Jesus gladly.

If happiness were the result of having *much,* then drugs, alcoholism, ulcers, and divorce would be less prevalent among the wealthy in our society. To the contrary, great treasure without reverence for God only produces turmoil and dissipation.

The Bible warns that *". . . the love of money is a root of all kinds of evil."* (1 Timothy 6:10a) If a root of a man's sin is materialism, then increasing his income will only *add* to his problem. The key to enjoying prosperity is not to be found in prosperity itself! Rather, it comes from the fulfillment of *seeing* God accomplish His will through the means which He has placed in your hands.

Make this your goal: love God, not money, and do not covet the lifestyle of those around you who love money. Jesus said, *". . . seek first His kingdom and His righteousness; and all these things shall be added to you."* (Matthew 6:33, KJV)

Good news! When you have enthroned Christ as Lord and have acknowledged His ownership of your life, your joy will be *equally great,* whether you have little or much of this world's goods!

Scriptural Insight	*Prayer*

Application: *I will* . . .

QUIET TIME 24

Read Matthew 13:44-46

Jesus said the kingdom of heaven is like a costly treasure; something of supreme quality, worth everything one owns. On another occasion, He referred to His *teachings* as pearls and warned His disciples not to give things of value to those who were spiritually unprepared to receive them. It was for this reason that the Lord so frequently said, *"If anyone has ears to hear, let him hear."* By that He meant, "If you can appreciate the value of spiritual truth, then listen to what I am about to say." Today that same challenge is ours every time we read the Bible or hear a sermon.

A famous fable tells of three men traveling in a desert by night. Under the starlight they met a stranger. He told them they would be both glad and sorry if they took his advice and filled their pockets and saddle-bags with the stones from a nearby river. The men were somewhat curious, but also quite skeptical; so when they reached the river, they took only a few of the stones. The next morning, they were "both glad and sorry," just as the man had said. The stones had turned into exquisite *pearls!* They were glad about the ones they had taken, but *sorry* about the ones they had left behind.

The cost of gaining spiritual insight has nothing to do with money. *Time* is the "price tag" for this investment of lasting value.

Timothy: You will notice that there are no more Scriptural insight, prayer, or application blanks at the bottom of your page. You may now start using the blanks provided in your *Spiritual Journal* in the Quiet Time Section on page 20.

QUIET TIME 25

Read 2 Timothy 3:16 & 17

God actually inspired the writing of the Bible. The term "inspired," or "God-breathed," means that it came from the mouth of God – and was what He wanted written. These verses present four valuable ministries of the Bible:

1. *Teaching* - It shows you God's plan for your life.
2. *Reproof* - It calls you to account when you sin.
3. *Correction* - It shows you how to correct your mistakes.
4. *Training in righteousness* - It shows you how to avoid sin in the future.

When you read the Bible on Monday, you may need *correction* because of a poor decision. However, on Tuesday you might be ready for God to *teach* you something totally fresh.

If you lived a hundred years and read the Bible every day, it would always be current. Billy Graham once said he had prayed about certain passages for 25 years and still did not fully understand their meaning; however, when the Lord knew he needed an explanation, the meaning of that passage would blossom like a beautiful flower whose season had finally come.

The Bible claims to be God's Word, and it has lived up to that claim across the centuries. Give it the sacred and holy place of honor that it rightfully deserves. Jesus said, *"Heaven and earth will pass away, but My words will never pass away."* (Matthew 24:35, NIV)

QUIET TIME 26

Read 2 Corinthians 9:6-13

Money is only a touchy subject to those who think they own it! The Bible reminds us that *"The earth is the Lord's, and all it contains, the world, and those who dwell in it."* (Psalm 24:1)

This simply means the clothes on your back, the car you drive, your house, the money in your bank account, and the very ground you walk upon are all His! Once this is understood, the ministry of giving is automatically seen in a whole new light.

God is merely allowing you and me the privilege of becoming involved in something which He deeply enjoys!

God is a giver, and as your Father, He wants you to become like Him. He gives bountifully, and He wants to teach you how to enjoy that same freedom.

He wants to "multiply your seed for sowing" and enrich your life through generous giving. The Bible says, *". . . God is able to make all grace abound to you, that . . . you may have an abundance for every good deed."* (2 Corinthians 9:8)

Do you still give *grudgingly*? Why? It shouldn't be hard to give away something that was *never* yours in the first place! Ask the Lord to remind you that you *own* nothing, and then begin trusting Him for real *joy* in giving.

Pause to look at your checkbook stubs; they will tell you volumes. The Bible says, *". . . where your treasure is, there will your heart be also."* (Matthew 6:21) Giving is the practical measure of our desire to become like our heavenly Father.

QUIET TIME 27

Read 1 Peter 5:8 & 9

Although Satan is a *defeated enemy* awaiting his final destruction, he still has *temporary power* to influence the lives of Christians and lost people here on earth. Peter describes him as *"a roaring lion,"* aggressively seeking his prey. In today's context, with blatant pornography, a soaring crime rate, profanity in the media, and the ever-present threat of war, his presence and activity are more evident than ever.

God's Word in this circumstance is – *"Resist the devil and he will flee from you."* (James 4:7b) You may be thinking, "How can this be done?" We are no match for Satan in our own strength, but with God's power working in and through us, we can indeed *". . .stand firm against the schemes of the devil."* (Ephesians 6:11b) Romans 8:31b boldly declares, *"If God be for us, who can be against us?"* (KJV) Like most bullies, Satan will cower in the face of a serious fight. Historically, it is Christians who have taken a stand on social and moral issues. We have been called to be salt and light in society!

On a personal level, you can decide *in advance* to say "no" to Satan's temptations as you daily reaffirm this decision. Resisting temptation will become a lifestyle. Each victory will become the foundation for added spiritual growth.

QUIET TIME 28

Read Philippians 1:6 three times.

When you received Christ as your Lord – you stepped into God's will. Now He wants to do something of lasting value in and through your life. His divine objective is to keep you *in a process* of positive change until you reach your full potential. Based on this truth, someone has said, "God loves us just the way we are, but He loves us *too* much to leave us that way!"

Paul expresses the same assurance, *". . . being confident of this, that He who began a good work in you will carry it on to completion . . ."* (Philippians 1:6a, NIV)

"For we are His workmanship, created in Christ Jesus for good works, which God prepared beforehand, that we should walk in them." (Ephesians 2:10) This means all of us were made for ministry! Each and every person has the capacity to say "yes" or "no" to that destiny.

You have already made life's biggest and most important decision, but living in daily obedience to God's plan requires a second kind of commitment – the eagerness to *keep on growing.* Said another way, your fulfillment will be as complete as your willingness to let Him complete His "good work" in your life.

Have you ever marvelled at the beauty of a butterfly? He begins life as a slow, earthbound caterpillar, then is transformed by a process called *metamorphosis.* In the same way, when you said "Yes" to Christ, God began the process of *spiritual metamorphosis* in you. Meditate on this fact: slowly but surely, you are being changed to resemble the inner beauty of His Son, Jesus Christ!

QUIET TIME 29

Read Philippians 4:15-20

The Christians to whom Paul wrote had recently sent him gifts to assist in his ministry. Paul commended them for their generosity, which was *"pleasing to God."* He also reminded them that God would meet all their needs.

You can take comfort in knowing that God will supply your personal *"daily bread"* just as He provided for the Christians in Philippi. That does not mean you can be lazy or wait for a gift to be dropped out of the sky. It does mean that if you are responsible and obedient to God, you can depend on Him to take care of you.

Faith is trusting. Trust in His sufficiency, even when you cannot see how all your needs will be provided!

A parent understands that a child needs food, clothing, and shelter, so all of these things are provided. A small child does not think about where his next meal will come from or what clothing he will wear. Though he may never realize it, he is totally dependent upon his parents.

The picture becomes clear when you stop to look at it this way: just as an earthly parent takes pleasure in meeting his child's needs, so our heavenly Father takes pleasure in meeting ours.

QUIET TIME 30

Read 1 Thessalonians 5:19-28

Paul says, *"Now may the God of peace Himself sanctify you entirely; and may your spirit and soul and body be preserved complete, without blame at the coming of our Lord Jesus Christ. Faithful is He who calls you, and He also will bring it to pass."* (1 Thessalonians 5:23-24)

The same God who called you to salvation is in the process of making you holy. The Bible calls this *"sanctification"* or *"being conformed to the image of Christ."* Salvation has three tenses:

Past Tense	Present Tense	Future Tense
Your spirit was saved when you accepted Christ and were born again spiritually.	Your soul (or mind) *is being* saved daily as you are changed by the indwelling Christ.	Your body *will be* saved when it is transformed at Christ's glorious return.

Salvation began with an event called conversion, but each day your thought life, your home life, your school life, your vocational life, and your religious life are all being saved from what they would have been without His presence in your heart.

As if *this* were not enough, God has even more in store: In His kingdom, your body will at last be perfect and beyond the reach of pain, aging, or sin. How can this be true? Because the God who made you willed it to be so and committed Himself to *"bring it to pass."*

Timothy: Now that you have finished these Quiet Time readings, you will start receiving your Scriptural insights from the Bible only. First read pages 6 & 7 of your *Spiritual Journal*. These pages will show you *how* to continue having an effective daily Quiet Time from the Scriptures. Next, turn to page 109 in your *Timothy's Guide*. This Guide shows you *where to read* to continue enjoying your daily Quiet Times.

QUIET TIME READING GUIDE

"Thy word is a lamp to my feet, and a light to my path."
(Psalm 119:105)

Review pages 6 & 7 in your *Spiritual Journal* before you begin. Read the Scriptures with personal application in mind. As you read each morning, come before the Lord with these prayerful attitudes:

Petition: Lord, help me to . . .

Adoration: Lord, You are . . .

Thanksgiving: Lord, thank You for . . .

Confession: Lord, please forgive me for . . .

Use the notetaking section of your *Spiritual Journal* to record any questions about passages which you find difficult to understand during your daily Quiet Times. Ask your Discipler to answer these questions during your next session. Start by reading Ephesians 1:1-14 during your first daily Quiet Time. Continue reading successive passages. You may wish to break these reading segments into smaller portions by stopping at each new Scriptural insight which you find. May you continue to grow spiritually as you let God mold your character through His Word!

Ephesians

1:1 - 14
1:15 - 23
2:1 - 10
2:11 - 22
3:1 - 13
3:14 - 21
4:1 - 16
4:17 - 32
5:1 - 21
5:22 - 33
6:1 - 9
6:10 - 24

Philippians

1:1 - 11
1:12 - 30
2:1 - 18
2:19 - 30
3:1 - 11
3:12 - 21
4:1 - 9
4:10 - 23

Colossians

1:1 - 14
1:15 - 23
1:24 - 29
2:1 - 12
2:13 - 23
3:1 - 17
3:18 - 25
4:1 - 6
4:7 - 18

1 Thessalonians

1:1 - 10
2:1 - 12
2:13 - 20
3: 1 - 13
4:1 - 12
4:13 - 18
5:1 - 11
5:12 - 28

2 Thessalonians

1:1 - 12
2:1 - 12
2:13 - 17
3:1 - 15
3:16 - 18

1 Timothy

1:1 - 11
1:12 - 20
2: 1 - 15
3:1 - 16
4:1 - 16
5:1 - 10
5:11 - 25
6:1 - 10
6:11 - 21

2 Timothy

1:1 - 18
2:1 - 13
2:14 - 26
3:1 - 9
3:10 - 17
4:1 - 8
4:9 -22

Titus	2 Peter
1:1 - 16	1:1 - 11
2:1 - 15	1:12 - 21
3:1 - 15	2:1 - 12
	2:13 - 22
Philemon	3:1 - 18
1:1 - 25	
	1 John
James	1:1 - 10
1: 1 - 18	2:1 - 14
1:19 - 27	2:15 - 29
2:1 - 13	3:1 - 10
2:14 - 26	3:11 - 24
3:1 - 12	4:1 - 6
3:13 - 18	4:7 - 21
4:1 - 12	5:1 - 12
4:13 - 17	5:13 - 21
5:1 - 12	
5:13 - 20	**2 John**
	1:1 - 13
1 Peter	
1:1 - 12	**3 John**
1:13 - 25	1:1 - 14
2:1 - 12	
2:13 - 25	**Jude**
3:1 - 7	1:1 - 16
3:8 - 22	1:17 - 25
4:1 - 11	
4:12 - 19	
5:1 - 14	

After you have completed these Quiet Time reading segments, you can enjoy reading the rest of the New Testament using the reading schedule on page 88 of your *Spiritual Journal*. Start in Matthew.

"And let us not lose heart in doing good, for in due time we shall reap if we do not grow weary." (Galatians 6:9)

RESOURCE SECTION

Please call (800) 880-1350 or FAX (800) 880-8465 for current discounted prices. You can also visit us on the World Wide Web at WWW.IEA.ORG.

Scripture Memory Packet (Living Word)
> Color-coded cards covering six topics: New Creations in Christ, Trials and Temptations, Abiding in Christ, Holy Behavior, Spreading the Good News, and Discipleship. Available in NIV, NASB, KJV, and NKJV.

Victory Scripture Memory Series (Word)
> This two booklet system covers the topics of Discipleship and Spiritual Growth. Each book contains verses for 26 weeks and is available in KJV and NASB.

Steps to Peace with God (Grason) 25 booklets per pack.
Bridge to Life (NavPress) 50 booklets per pack.
Assured of Heaven **Cassettes** (Word) A direct presentation of the Gospel on cassette.

Books:
> *Be Loyal* - **Matthew** (Warren Wiersbe) (Scripture Press)
> *Everyday Evangelism* (Billie Hanks Jr.) (Word)
> *If You Love Me* (Billie Hanks Jr.) (Word)

The Gift of Giving (Wayne Watts) (IEA)
Discipleship (Billie Hanks, Bill Shell) (Zondervan)

Spiritual Journals:

Spiritual Journal **with Suede Jacket** (Navy)

Spiritual Journal **Refills** 4 Journals per pack.

ADDITIONAL NOTES and PRAYER REQUESTS

ADDITIONAL NOTES and PRAYER REQUESTS

ADDITIONAL NOTES and PRAYER REQUESTS

_____

_____

_____

_____

_____

_____

_____

_____

_____

_____

_____

_____

_____

_____

_____

_____

_____

_____

_____

_____

_____

ADDITIONAL NOTES and PRAYER REQUESTS